Jumpstarters for Geometry

Short Daily Warm-ups for the Classroom

By
VICKY SHIOTSU

COPYRIGHT © 2007 Mark Twain Media, Inc.

ISBN 978-1-58037-399-9

Printing No. CD-404058

Mark Twain Media, Inc., Publishers
Distributed by Carson-Dellosa Publishing Company, Inc.

The purchase of this book entitles the buyer to reproduce the student pages for classroom use only. Other permissions may be obtained by writing Mark Twain Media, Inc., Publishers.

All rights reserved. Printed in the United States of America.

M000166340

Table of Contents

Introduction to the Teacher

Just as physical warm-ups help athletes prepare for more strenuous types of activity, mental warm-ups help students prepare for the day's lesson while reviewing what they have previously learned. The short warm-up activities presented in this book provide teachers and parents with activities to help students develop and reinforce geometry-related skills. Each page contains five warm-ups—one for each day of the school week. Used at the beginning of class, warm-ups help students focus on geometry-related concepts.

Geometry is the branch of mathematics that deals with the measurement, properties, and relationships of points, lines, angles, surfaces, and solids. The warm-up activities in this book move from the most basic lines to more complex concepts such as angles, polygons, symmetry, transformations, perimeter, area, volume, circles, solid figures, and the coordinate plane.

Although the warm-ups have been arranged to present more basic topics up front, you do not need to give them to your class in sequential order. Choose the pages in the order that best fits your curriculum needs. In addition, the five warm-ups that are on the same page may be presented in any order, since they all relate to the same topic or skill.

Suggestions for use:

- Copy and cut apart one page each week. Give students one warm-up activity each day at the beginning of class.
- Give each student a copy of the entire page to complete day by day. Students can keep the completed pages in a three-ring binder or folder to use as a resource.
- Make transparencies of individual warm-ups and complete the activities as a group.
- Provide additional copies of warm-ups in your learning center for students to complete at random when they have a few extra minutes.
- Keep some warm-ups on hand to use as fill-ins when the class has a few extra minutes before lunch or dismissal.

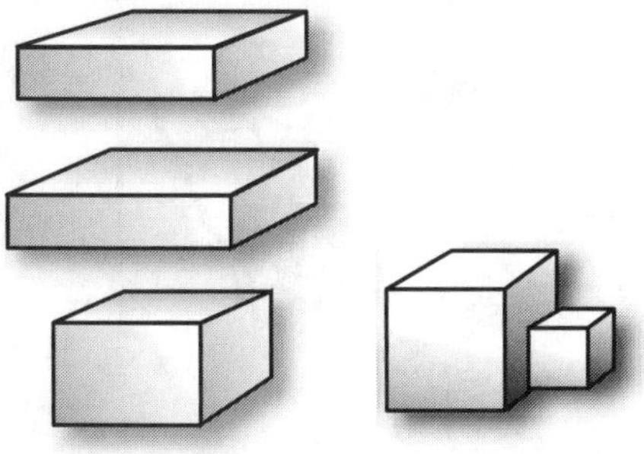

Geometry Warm-ups: Lines, Rays, and Line Segments

Name/Date ____________________

Lines, Rays, and Line Segments 1

Label each figure as a **line**, **ray**, or **line segment**.

A.  ____________________

B.  ____________________

C.  ____________________

D.  ____________________

Name/Date ____________________

Lines, Rays, and Line Segments 2

How many line segments are in the picture?

__________ Name them.

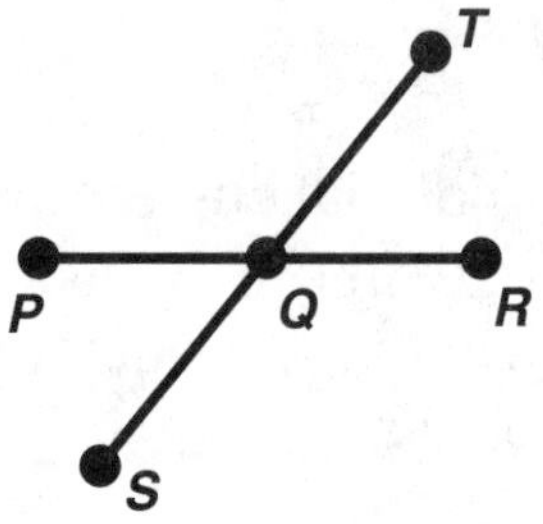

____

____

____

Name/Date ____________________

Lines, Rays, and Line Segments 3

Use letters and symbols to label each figure.

This line is $\overleftrightarrow{AB}$ or $\overleftrightarrow{BA}$.

A.  ____________________

B.  ____________________

C.  ____________________

Name/Date ____________________

Lines, Rays, and Line Segments 4

Are the following statements true or false?

A. A line segment has only one endpoint. ____________________

B. A line has two endpoints. ____________________

C. A ray goes on without end in one direction. ____________________

D. A line goes on without end in two directions. ____________________

Name/Date ____________________

Lines, Rays, and Line Segments 5

Look at the picture. Name the following figures.

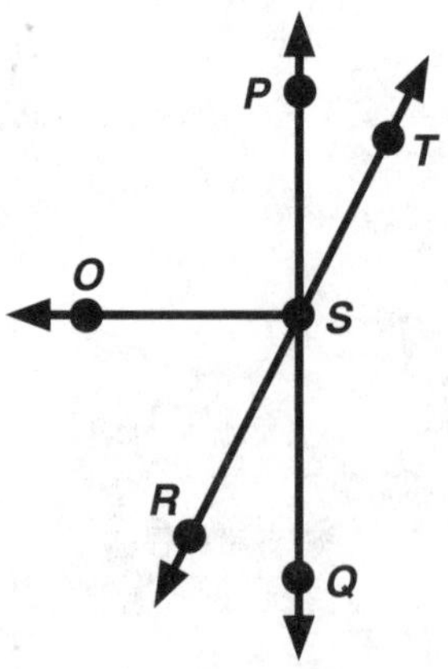

A. two lines ____________________

B. five rays ____________________

C. two line segments that contain point Q ____________________

© Mark Twain Media, Inc., Publishers

Geometry Warm-ups: Classifying Angles

Name/Date ____________

Classifying Angles 1

Write three names for each angle. Use symbols and letters. (Examples: ∠*PQR,* ∠*RQP,* ∠*Q*)

A. 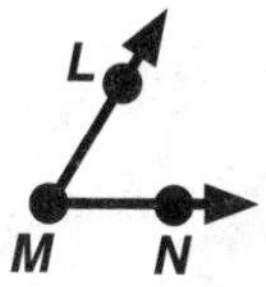

B. 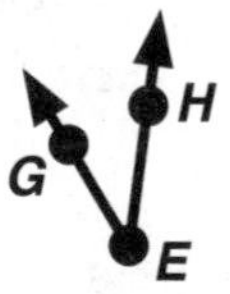

C. 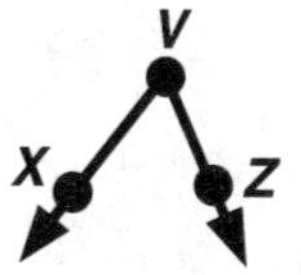

________ ________ ________

________ ________ ________

________ ________ ________

Name/Date ____________

Classifying Angles 2

A. What do you call the point that is common to the two sides of an angle? ________

B. Can angle *XYZ* also be named angle *ZYX*? Explain. ________

____

C. Can angle *XYZ* also be called angle *YZX*? Explain. ________

____

Name/Date ____________

Classifying Angles 3

Write **acute**, **obtuse**, **right**, or **straight** to describe the angles.

A. 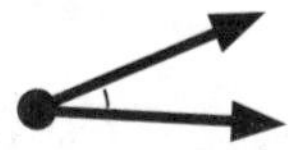

____

B. 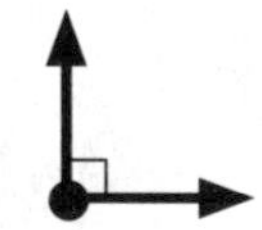

____

C. 

____

D. 

____

Name/Date ____________

Classifying Angles 4

Write **acute**, **obtuse**, **right**, or **straight**.

A. Which angle measures 90 degrees?

____

B. Which angle is greater than 90 degrees but less than 180 degrees? ________

C. Which angle is less than 90 degrees?

____

D. Which angle equals 180 degrees?

____

Name/Date ____________

Classifying Angles 5

Use the figure at right to answer these questions.

A. Name an acute angle. ________

B. Name a right angle. ________

C. Name a straight angle. ________

D. Name an obtuse angle. ________

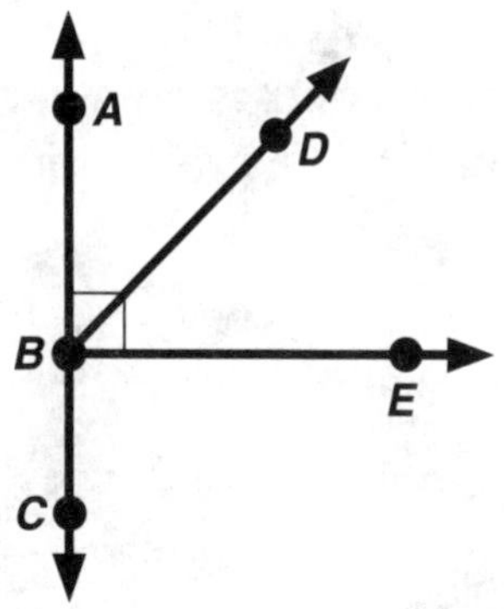

© Mark Twain Media, Inc., Publishers

Geometry Warm-ups: Measuring and Drawing Angles

Name/Date ______________________________

Measuring and Drawing Angles 1

Write the missing numbers.

A. A straight angle measures ______ degrees.

B. A right angle measures ______ degrees.

C. An acute angle measures less than ______ degrees but greater than ______ degrees.

D. An obtuse angle measures greater than ______ degrees but less than ______ degrees.

Name/Date ______________________________

Measuring and Drawing Angles 2

Use a protractor to measure the angles.

A. ______°

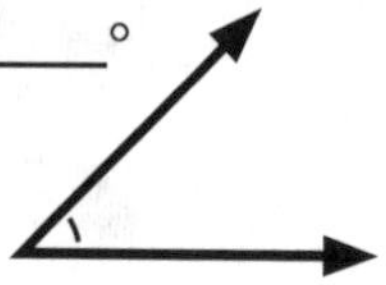

B. ______°

C. ______°

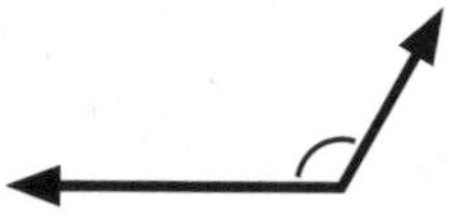

Name/Date ______________________________

Measuring and Drawing Angles 3

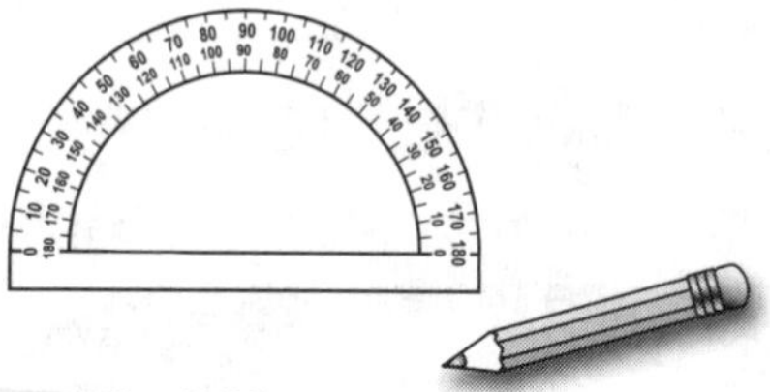

Use a protractor to draw the angles with the following measures.

A. 30° B. 60° C. 135° D. 90°

Name/Date ______________________________

Measuring and Drawing Angles 4

Draw the following angles on a separate sheet of paper. Then use a protractor to measure your angles.

A. an acute angle

B. an obtuse angle

C. a right angle

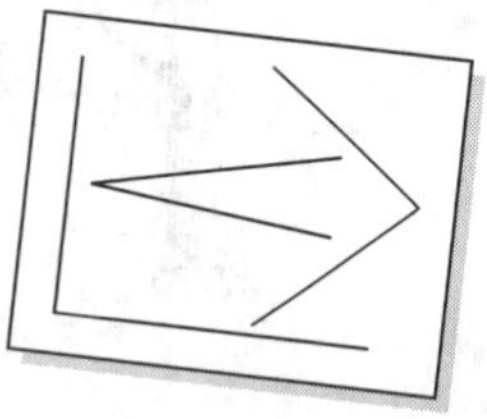

Name/Date ______________________________

Measuring and Drawing Angles 5

Use a protractor to measure angles *A, B, C,* and *D*. Write **acute**, **obtuse**, or **right** beside each measure.

A. ______________________

B. ______________________

C. ______________________

D. ______________________

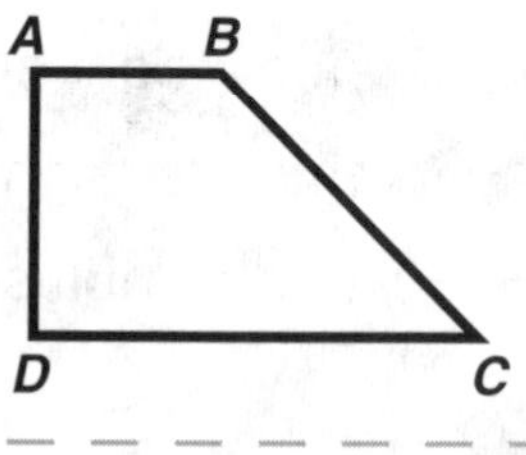

Geometry Warm-ups: Classifying Pairs of Lines

Name/Date ____________________

Classifying Pairs of Lines 1

Write **parallel**, **perpendicular**, or **intersecting** to describe each set of lines.

A. ______________

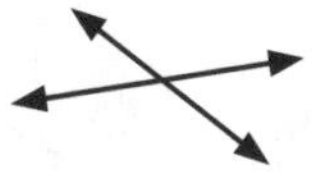

B. ______________

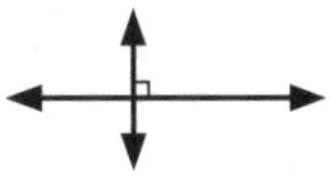

C. ______________

D. ______________

Name/Date ____________________

Classifying Pairs of Lines 2

Draw on a separate sheet of paper.

A. Draw a pair of parallel lines.

B. Draw a pair of perpendicular lines.

C. Draw a pair of intersecting lines that are not perpendicular.

Name/Date ____________________

Classifying Pairs of Lines 3

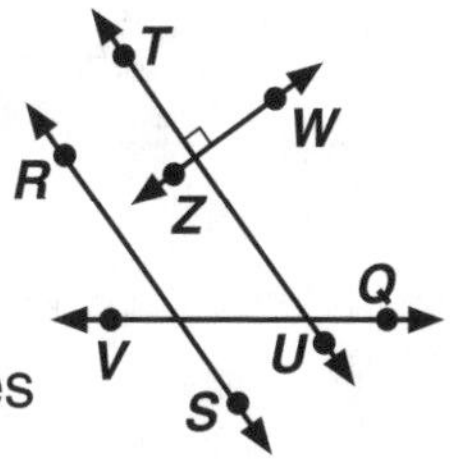

A. Name two parallel lines.

____

B. Name two perpendicular lines. ______________

C. Name two intersecting lines that are not perpendicular.

____

Name/Date ____________________

Classifying Pairs of Lines 4

Write "T" for true or "F" for false.

_____ A. Parallel lines never intersect.

_____ B. Some intersecting lines are perpendicular.

_____ C. Perpendicular lines rarely intersect.

_____ D. If two lines are perpendicular, then they are also parallel.

Name/Date ____________________

Classifying Pairs of Lines 5

Write **parallel**, **perpendicular**, or **intersecting** for each pair of lines.

A. $\overleftrightarrow{RU}$ and $\overleftrightarrow{TV}$ ______________

B. $\overleftrightarrow{SQ}$ and $\overleftrightarrow{RU}$ ______________

C. $\overleftrightarrow{RT}$ and $\overleftrightarrow{RU}$ ______________

D. $\overleftrightarrow{UV}$ and $\overleftrightarrow{SQ}$ ______________

E. $\overleftrightarrow{TV}$ and $\overleftrightarrow{QS}$ ______________

F. $\overleftrightarrow{VT}$ and $\overleftrightarrow{TR}$ ______________

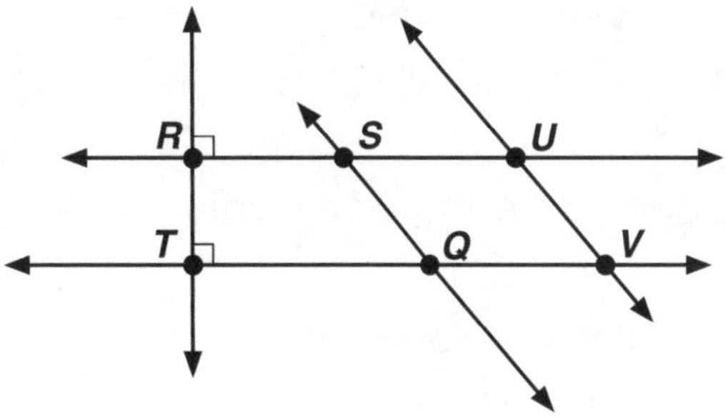

Geometry Warm-ups: Special Pairs of Angles

Name/Date ______________________________

Special Pairs of Angles 1

Write **vertical**, **complementary**, or **supplementary** to describe each pair of angles.

A. The sum of the measures of these two angles is 180 degrees. ____________________

B. These angles are always congruent.

____

C. The sum of the measures of these two angles is 90 degrees. ____________________

Name/Date ______________________________

Special Pairs of Angles 2

The angles in each pair are complementary. Write the missing angle measures.

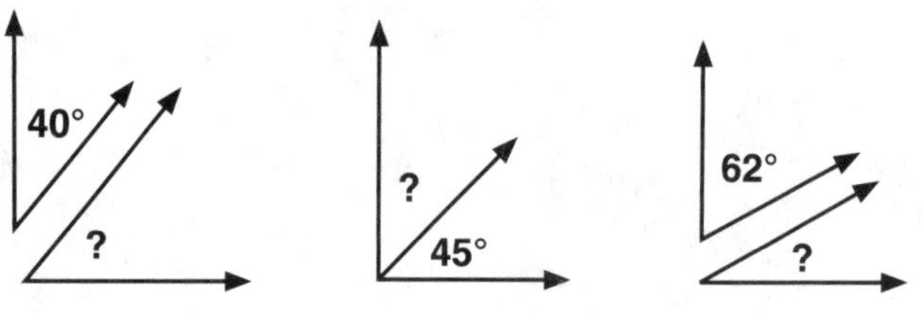

A. _____° B. _____° C. _____°

Name/Date ______________________________

Special Pairs of Angles 3

The angles in each pair are supplementary. Write the missing angle measures.

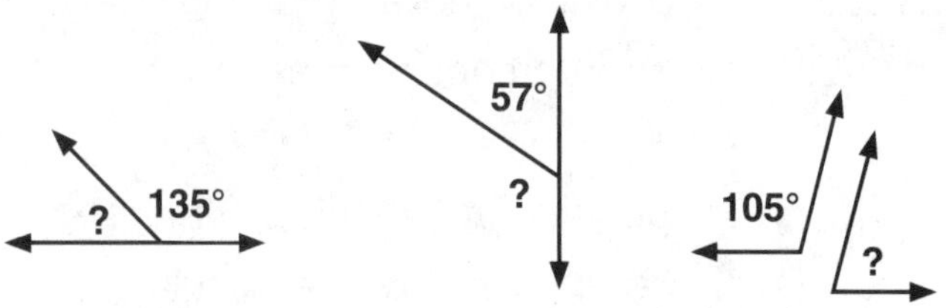

A. _____° B. _____° C. _____°

Name/Date ______________________________

Special Pairs of Angles 4

A. Two angles are vertical. One angle measures 112 degrees. The other measures _____ degrees.

B. Two angles are supplementary. One measures 97 degrees. The other measures _____ degrees.

C. Two angles are complementary. One angle measures 36 degrees. The other measures _____ degrees.

Name/Date ______________________________

Special Pairs of Angles 5

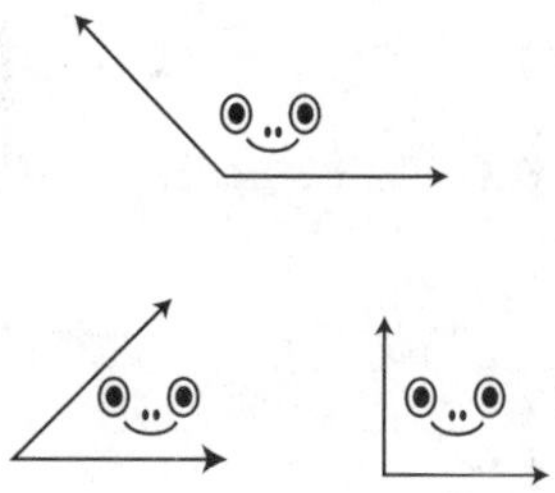

A. Two complementary angles have the same measure. What is their angle measure? __________

B. Two supplementary angles have the same measure. What is their angle measure? __________

C. Two angles are complementary. One angle is twice the other. What are the angle measures? ______________

D. Two angles are supplementary. One angle measures 10 degrees more than the other. What are the angle measures? ______________

Geometry Warm-ups: Identifying Polygons

Name/Date ____________________

Identifying Polygons 1

Are these figures polygons?

A. ______ 

B. ______ 

C. ______ 

D. ______ 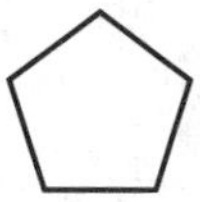

E. ______ 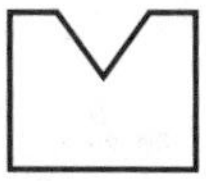

F. ______ 

Name/Date ____________________

Identifying Polygons 2

How many sides, angles, and vertices do these polygons have?

	Sides	Angles	Vertices
A. pentagon	____	____	____
B. quadrilateral	____	____	____
C. octagon	____	____	____
D. hexagon	____	____	____

Name/Date ____________________

Identifying Polygons 3

Write the names of these polygons.

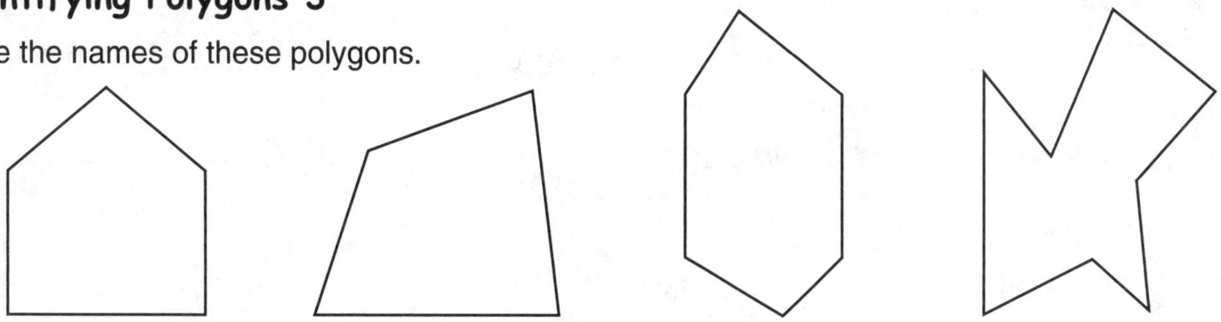

A. ____________ B. ____________ C. ____________ D. ____________

Name/Date ____________________

Identifying Polygons 4

A. Can a polygon have only 2 vertices? ______

Explain. ____________________

____

B. Is a circle a polygon? ______ Explain.

____

____

Name/Date ____________________

Identifying Polygons 5

A. Are all rectangles squares? ______ Explain.

____

____

B. Are all squares rectangles? ______ Explain.

____

____

____

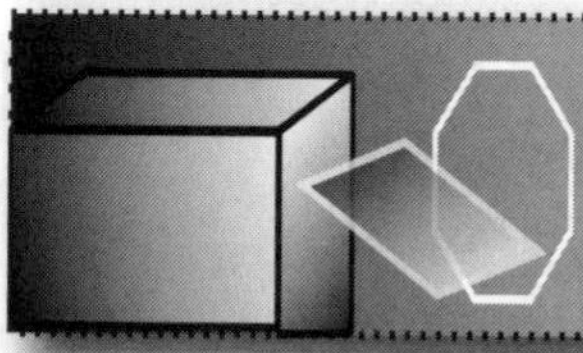

Geometry Warm-ups: Polygon Puzzles

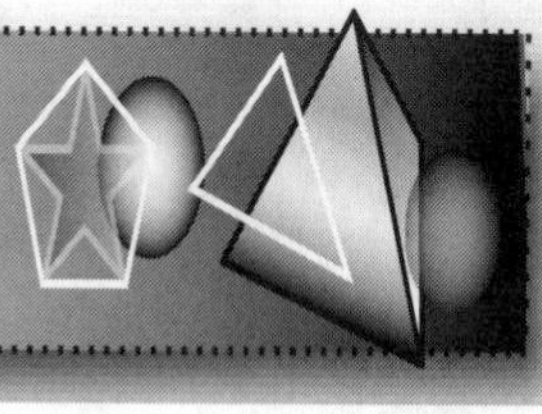

Name/Date ______________________

Polygon Puzzles 1

A. Draw two squares using only five lines.

B. Draw two squares using only six lines.

Name/Date ______________________

Polygon Puzzles 2

A. Draw two triangles that are the same size and shape using only four lines.

B. Draw two triangles that are the same size and shape using only five lines.

Name/Date ______________________

Polygon Puzzles 3

Suppose you were going to cut this rectangle in half along the lines.

How many different ways could you cut it? ________

Draw your answers in the space below.

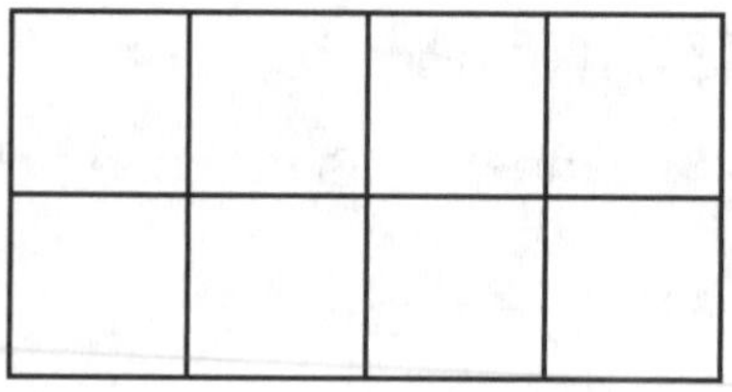

Name/Date ______________________

Polygon Puzzles 4

How many triangles are in this figure? ________

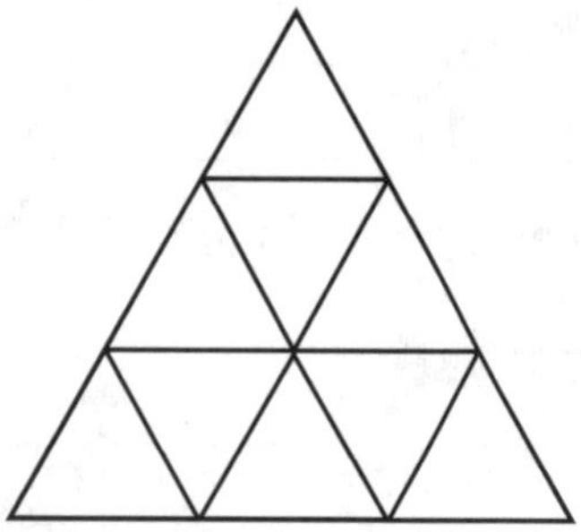

Name/Date ______________________

Polygon Puzzles 5

A. Draw two lines to divide the shape into three equal parts.

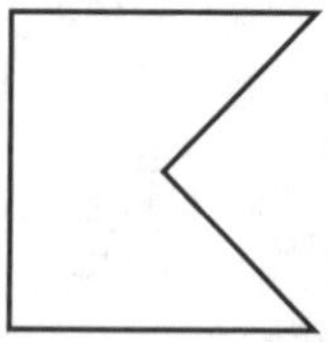

B. Connect the dots so that you get two squares.

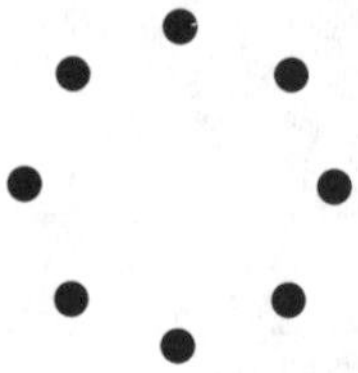

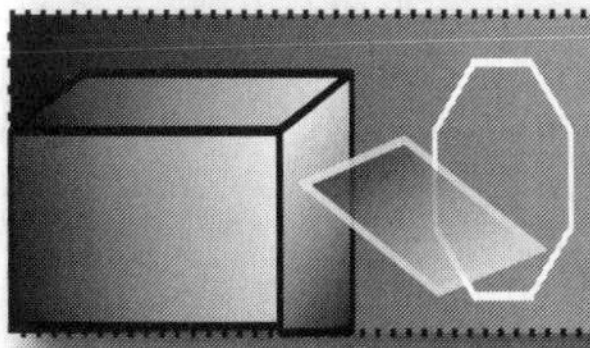

Geometry Warm-ups: Congruent Figures

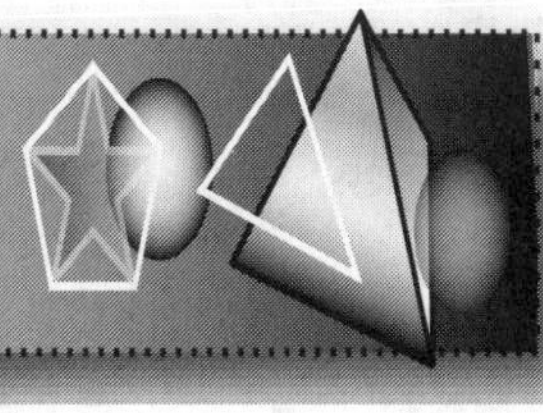

Name/Date ____________________

Congruent Figures 1

Are the two figures in each set congruent?

A. 

____

B. 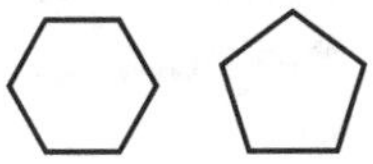

____

C. 

____

D. 

____

Name/Date ____________________

Congruent Figures 2

Which two figures in each row are congruent? Write the numbers.

A. ____________

B. ____________

C. ____________

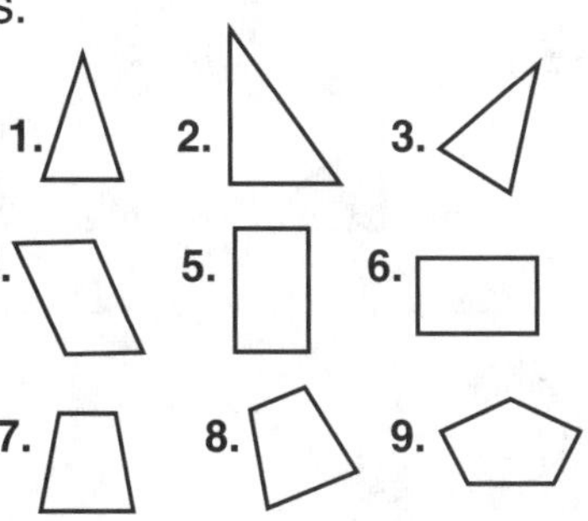

Name/Date ____________________

Congruent Figures 3

Triangle *ABC* is congruent to triangle *DEF*.

A. Which segment is congruent to $\overline{AB}$? ____________

B. Which segment is congruent to $\overline{BC}$? ____________

C. Which segment is congruent to $\overline{AC}$? ____________

D. Which angle is congruent to $\angle ABC$? ____________

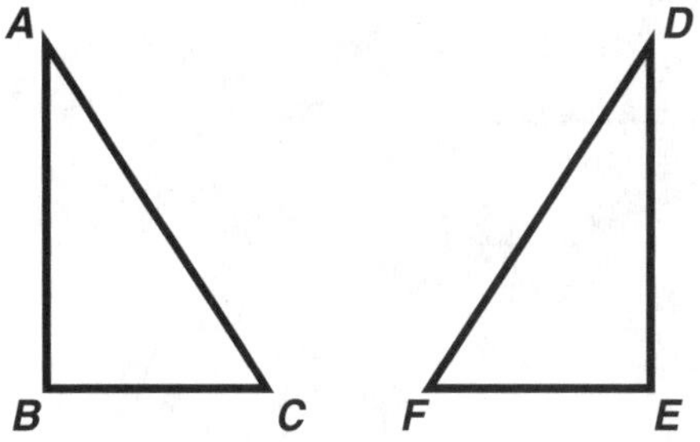

Name/Date ____________________

Congruent Figures 4

Draw on a separate sheet of paper.

A. Draw a triangle that has exactly two congruent sides.

B. Draw a triangle that has three congruent sides.

C. Draw a figure that has four sides. Make all the sides congruent. Do not make a square.

Name/Date ____________________

Congruent Figures 5

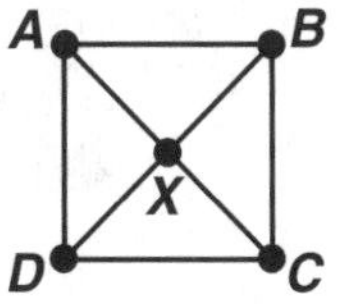

Use the square to do the following:

A. Name the triangles that are congruent to triangle *AXB*.

____

B. Name the segments that are congruent to $\overline{AC}$. ____________________

C. Which triangles are congruent to triangle *ADC*? ____________________

© Mark Twain Media, Inc., Publishers

Geometry Warm-ups: Similar Figures

Name/Date ______________________________

Similar Figures 1

Are the two figures in each set similar?

A. ________

B. ________

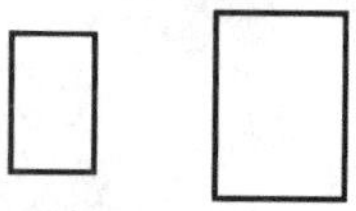

C. ________

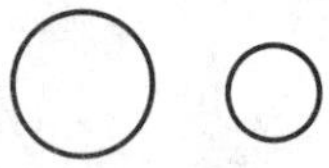

D. ________

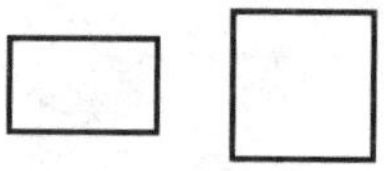

Name/Date ______________________________

Similar Figures 2

Which two figures in each row are similar? Write the numbers.

A. ________

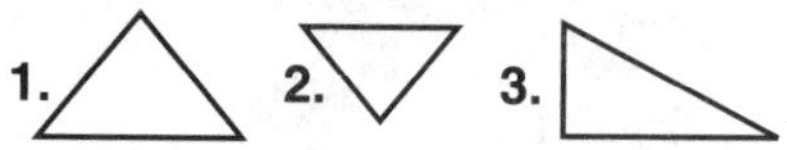

B. ________

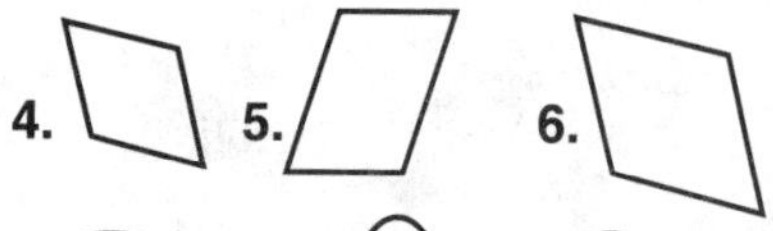

C. ________

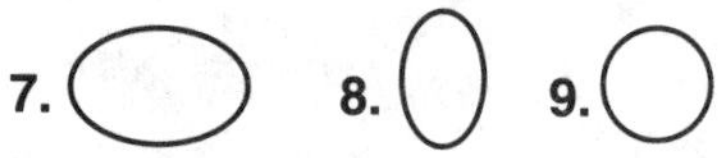

Name/Date ______________________________

Similar Figures 3

Find the four pairs of similar figures. Write their numbers on the lines.

A. ________

B. ________

C. ________

D. ________

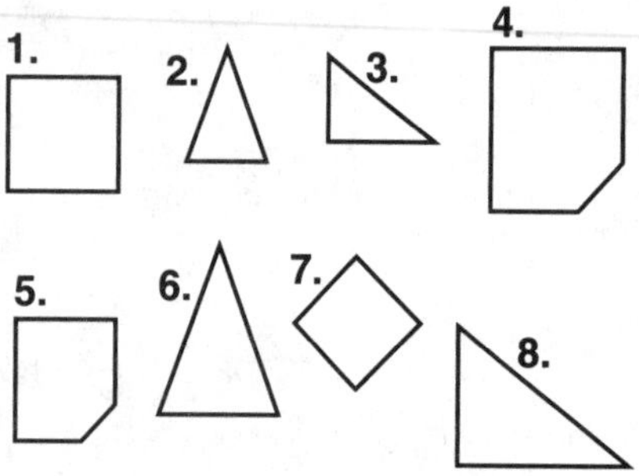

Name/Date ______________________________

Similar Figures 4

Write "T" for true or "F" for false.

_____ A. All squares are similar.

_____ B. All rectangles are similar.

_____ C. All triangles are similar.

_____ D. All circles are similar.

_____ E. All hexagons are similar.

Name/Date ______________________________

Similar Figures 5

The figures in each pair are similar. Find the missing lengths.

A. s = ______

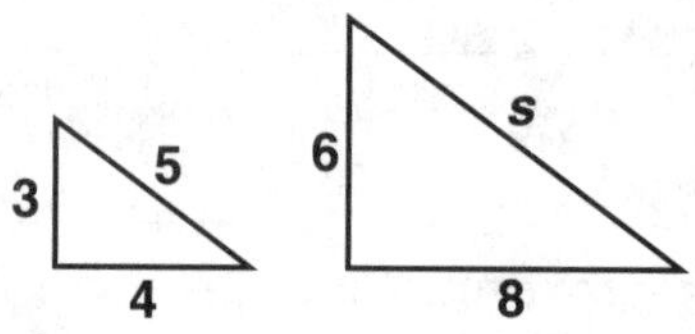

B. t = ______

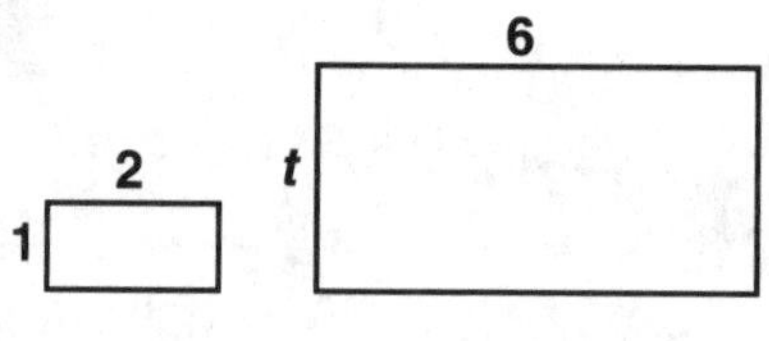

C. x = ______ y = ______

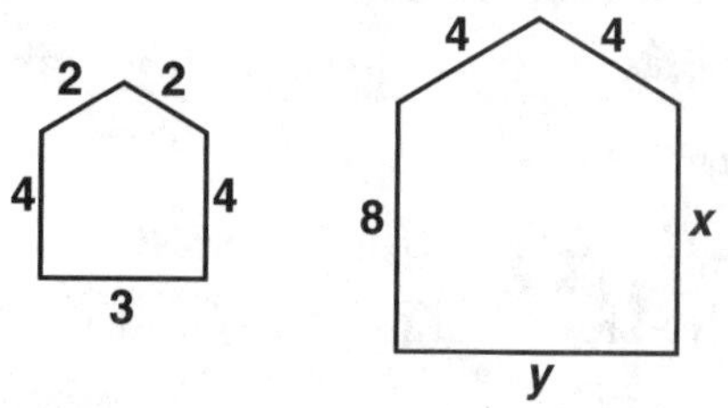

Geometry Warm-ups: Symmetrical Figures

Name/Date ______________________

Symmetrical Figures 1

Is the dashed line a line of symmetry?

A. ________

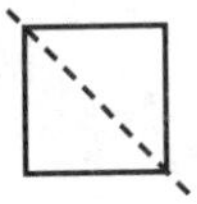

B. ________

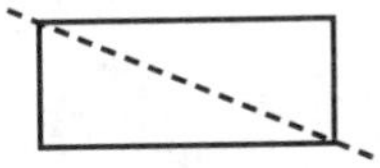

C. ________

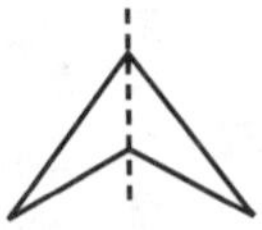

D. ________

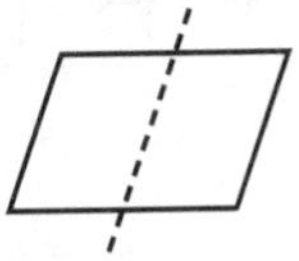

Name/Date ______________________

Symmetrical Figures 2

Is the letter symmetrical? Write "yes" or "no." If it is, draw the line of symmetry.

A. ________ O

B. ________ F

C. ________ T

D. ________ Z

E. ________ H

F. ________ V

Name/Date ______________________

Symmetrical Figures 3

Draw a line of symmetry through each figure.

A.

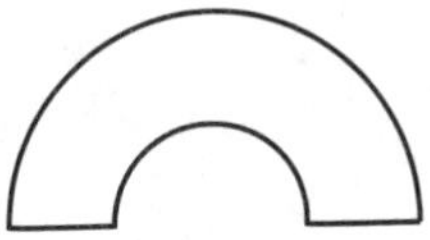

B.

C.

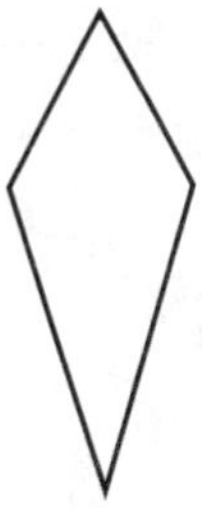

D.

E.

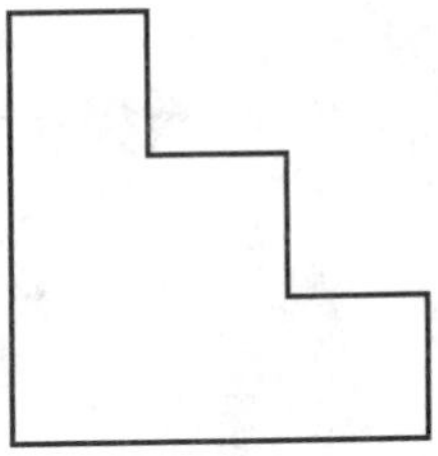

Name/Date ______________________

Symmetrical Figures 4

Write how many lines of symmetry each figure has. Then draw them.

A.

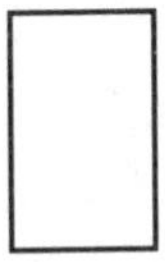

____

B.

____

C.

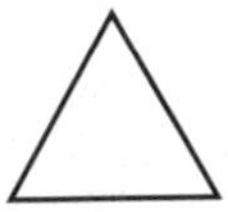

____

Name/Date ______________________

Symmetrical Figures 5

Complete the missing half of each design to find the missing words.

A. 

B. 

C. 

D. 

© Mark Twain Media, Inc., Publishers

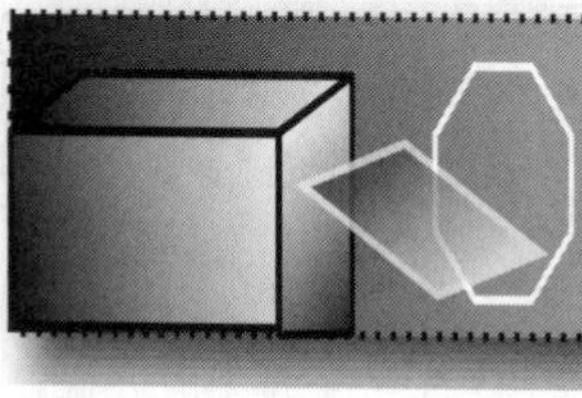

Geometry Warm-ups: Two Types of Symmetry

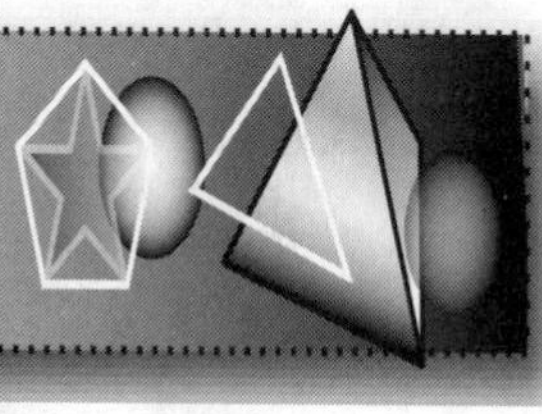

Name/Date ____________________

Two Types of Symmetry 1

Does the figure have line symmetry? If it does, draw the line of symmetry.

A. ________ 

B. ________ 

C. ________ 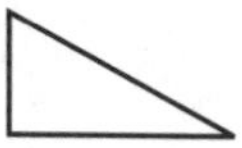

D. ________ 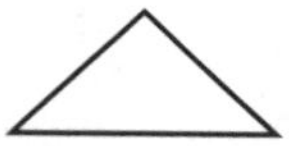

Name/Date ____________________

Two Types of Symmetry 2

Does the figure have rotational symmetry?

A. ________ 

B. ________ 

C. ________ 

D. ________ 

Name/Date ____________________

Two Types of Symmetry 3

Write **line**, **rotational**, or **both** to show what kind of symmetry each design has.

A. ________ 

B. ________ 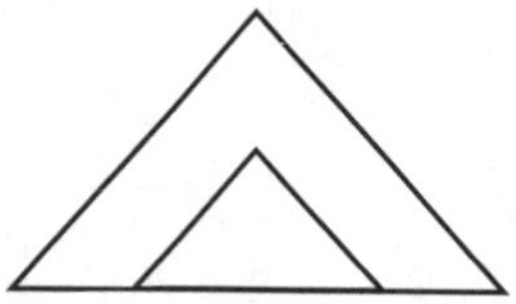

C. ________ 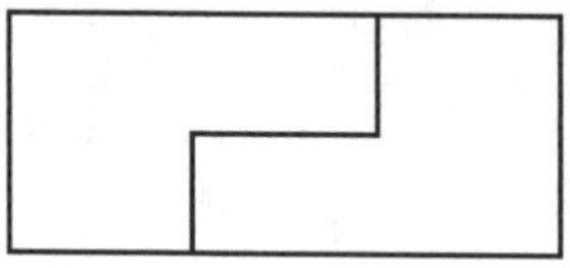

D. ________ 

Name/Date ____________________

Two Types of Symmetry 4

Look at each letter. Write **line**, **rotational**, or **both** to show what kind of symmetry it has.

A. ________
C

B. ________
X

C. ________
N

D. ________
M

Name/Date ____________________

Two Types of Symmetry 5

A. Draw a figure that has line symmetry.

B. Draw a figure that has rotational symmetry.

Geometry Warm-ups: Transformations

Name/Date ______________________

Transformations 1

A **reflection** flips a figure across a line. Draw the reflection of each figure below.

A. 

B. 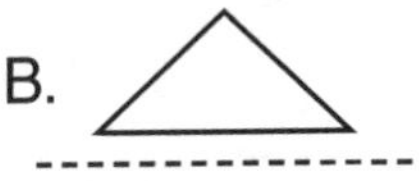

C. 

Name/Date ______________________

Transformations 2

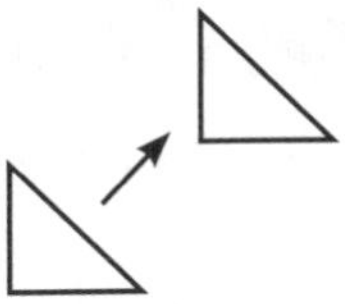

A **translation** slides a figure in a given direction. Draw the translation of each figure.

A. 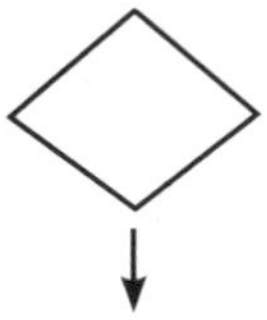

B. 

C. 

Name/Date ______________________

Transformations 3

A **rotation** turns a figure about a given point.

Draw a rotation of  .

A. a quarter turn

B. a half turn

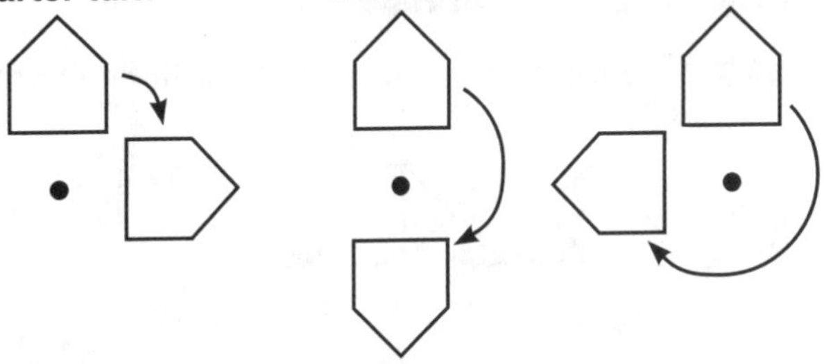

C. a three-quarters turn

Name/Date ______________________

Transformations 4

Write whether the transformation is a **reflection**, **translation**, or **rotation**.

A. 
____

B. 
____

C. 
____

Name/Date ______________________

Transformations 5

List the capital letters of the alphabet that remain the same when they are reflected across a vertical line.

____

____

____

© Mark Twain Media, Inc., Publishers

Geometry Warm-ups: Geometric Patterns

Name/Date ____________________

Geometric Patterns 1

Draw the next two figures in each pattern.

A. 

B. 

C. 

Name/Date ____________________

Geometric Patterns 2

How many squares are needed to make the seventh figure in the pattern? ______

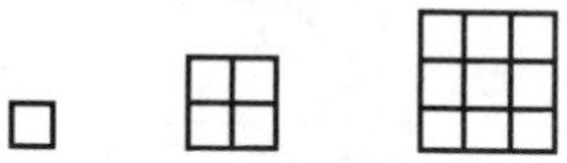

Describe how you found the answer. ______

______

______

Name/Date ____________________

Geometric Patterns 3

Color the shapes to extend each pattern. Then make up your own pattern for the last picture.

A. 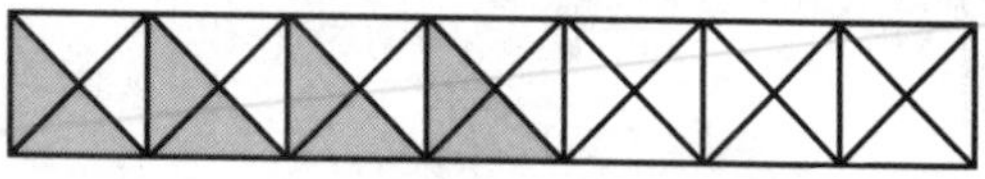

B. 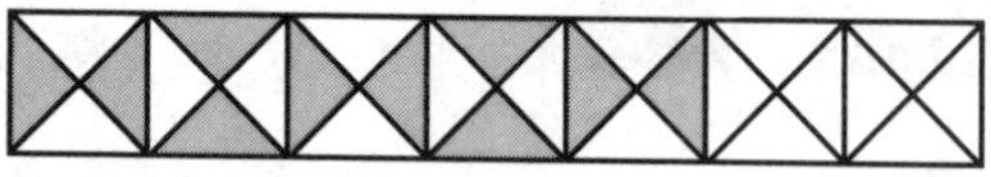

C. 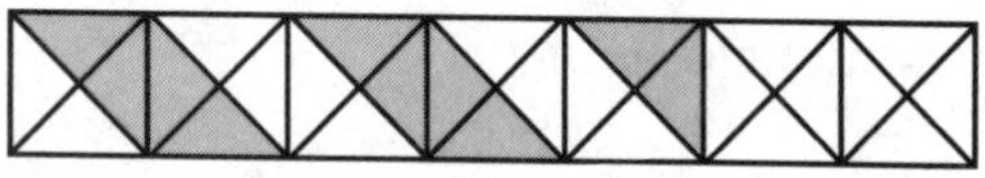

D. 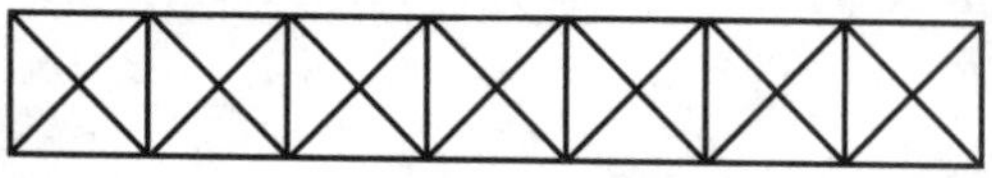

Name/Date ____________________

Geometric Patterns 4

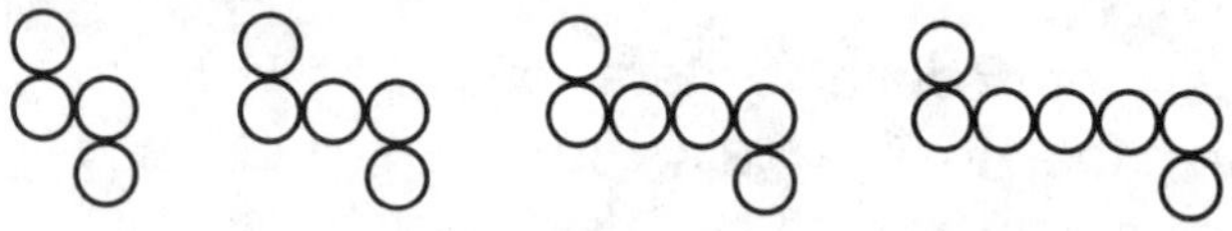

How many circles are needed for the tenth figure in the pattern? ______

How can you find out without using counters or drawing a picture? ______

______

______

Name/Date ____________________

Geometric Patterns 5

How many triangles are needed in all if you extend the pattern to eight rows? ______

Geometry Warm-ups: Classifying Triangles

Name/Date ______________________

Classifying Triangles 1

Write **equilateral**, **isosceles**, or **scalene** to describe each triangle.

A. 

B. 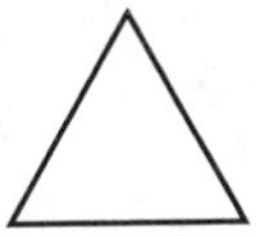

C. 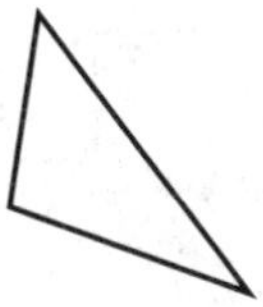

A. ________ B. ________ C. ________

Name/Date ______________________

Classifying Triangles 2

Write **acute**, **right**, or **obtuse** to describe each triangle.

A. 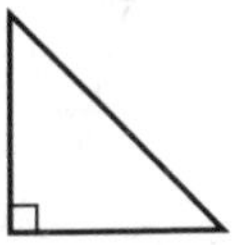

B. 

C. 

A. ________ B. ________ C. ________

Name/Date ______________________

Classifying Triangles 3

Match the words with their clues. You will not use two of the words.

equilateral	**isosceles**	**scalene**
right	**obtuse**	**acute**

A. No sides are the same length. ____________

B. One angle is 90°. ____________

C. At least two sides are equal. ____________

D. All angles are less than 90°. ____________

Name/Date ______________________

Classifying Triangles 4

Write **A** for always, **S** for sometimes, or **N** for never on the line next to each statement.

____ A. A right triangle is a scalene triangle.

____ B. An equilateral triangle is an isosceles triangle.

____ C. An isosceles triangle is a right triangle.

____ D. An equilateral triangle is obtuse.

Name/Date ______________________

Classifying Triangles 5

equilateral	**scalene**
isosceles	**right**
obtuse	**acute**

Write two words from the box to describe each triangle.

A. 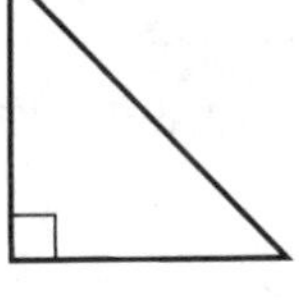

B. 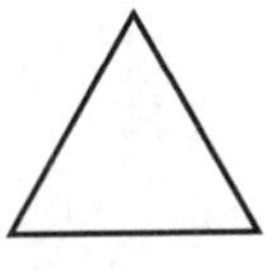

C. 

D. 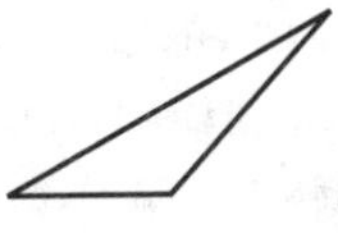

© Mark Twain Media, Inc., Publishers

Geometry Warm-ups: Classifying Quadrilaterals

Name/Date ______________________________

Classifying Quadrilaterals 1

Look at each figure. Is it a quadrilateral?

A. ________ B. ________ C. ________

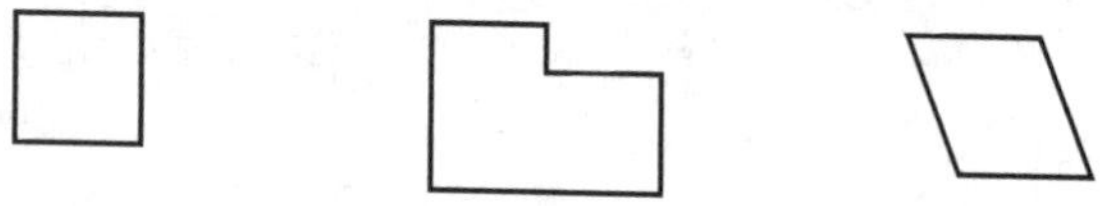

D. ________ E. ________ F. ________

Name/Date ______________________________

Classifying Quadrilaterals 2

Write the numbers of the figures that are trapezoids.

____

1. 2. 3. 4.

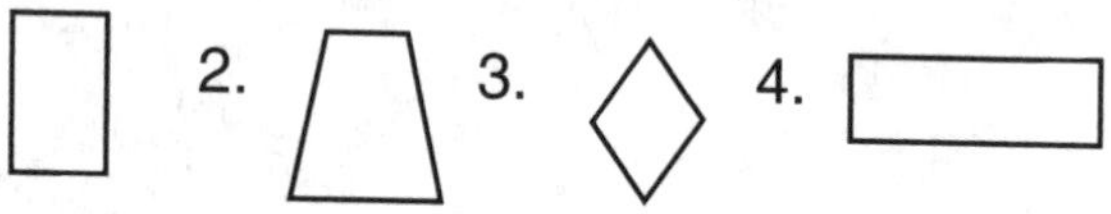

5. 6. 7. 8.

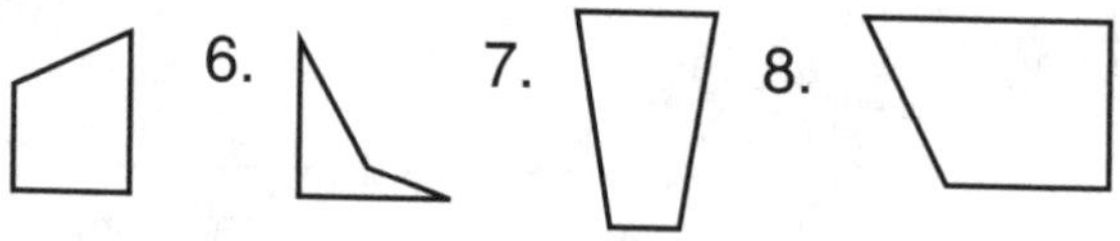

Name/Date ______________________________

Classifying Quadrilaterals 3

For each name, write the numbers of all the shapes that apply.

A. rhombus ______________________
B. rectangle ______________________
C. trapezoid ______________________
D. parallelogram ______________________
E. quadrilateral ______________________

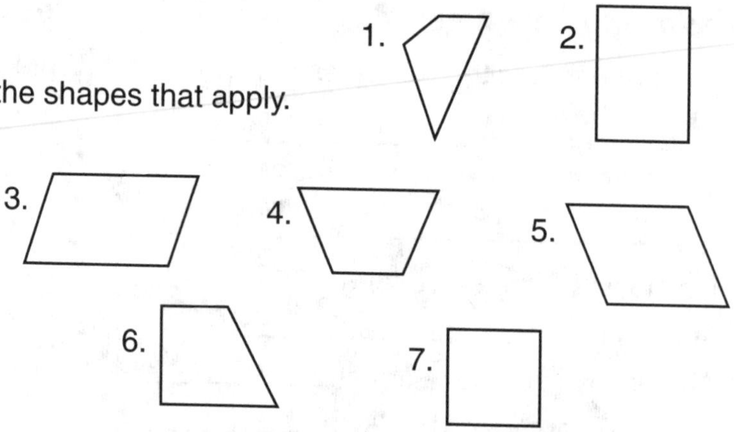

Name/Date ______________________________

Classifying Quadrilaterals 4

A. Draw a quadrilateral with exactly one pair of parallel lines.
B. Draw a quadrilateral with four congruent sides.
C. Draw a quadrilateral with two pairs of parallel sides and four right angles.

Name/Date ______________________________

Classifying Quadrilaterals 5

A. Are all squares rhombuses? ________
Explain. ______________________
____

B. Do all quadrilaterals have at least one pair of parallel sides? ________
Explain. ______________________
____
____

© Mark Twain Media, Inc., Publishers

Geometry Warm-ups: Classifying Parallelograms

Name/Date ______________________________

Classifying Parallelograms 1

Look at each figure. Is it a parallelogram?

A. ________

B. ________
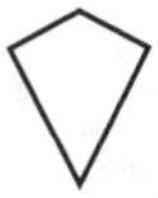

C. ________
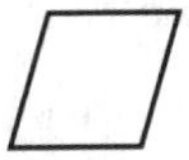

D. ________

E. ________
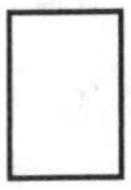

F. ________
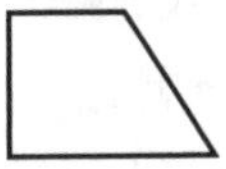

Name/Date ______________________________

Classifying Parallelograms 2

Write the names that match each clue. Use the words in the box.

rhombus rectangle square

A. has four congruent sides

____

B. has four right angles

____

C. has opposite sides that are congruent and parallel ______________________________

____

Name/Date ______________________________

Classifying Parallelograms 3

A. Are all rectangles parallelograms? ________

Explain. ______________________________

____

B. Are all quadrilaterals parallelograms? ________

Explain. ______________________________

____

____

Name/Date ______________________________

Classifying Parallelograms 4

The figure at the right is a parallelogram.

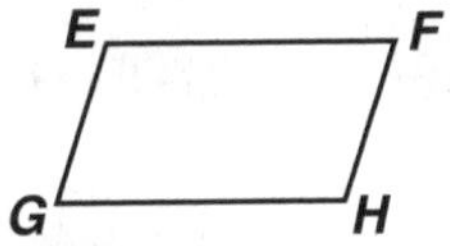

A. Which segments are congruent?

____

B. Which segments are parallel?

____

Name/Date ______________________________

Classifying Parallelograms 5

Figure *QRST* is a parallelogram. Write the names of all the other parallelograms in the picture.

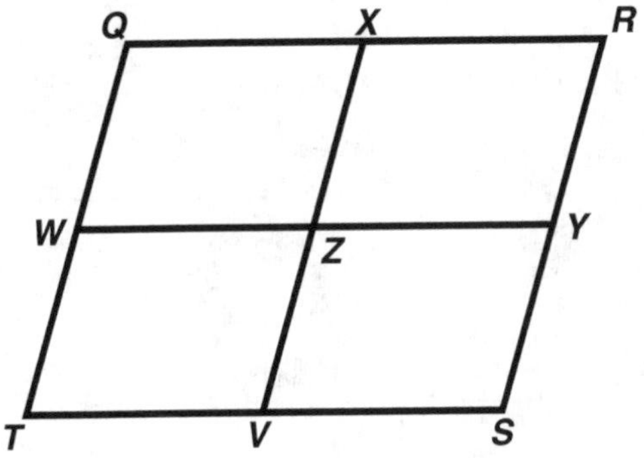

____

____

____

Geometry Warm-ups: Angle Measures of Triangles

Name/Date ____________________

Angle Measures of Triangles 1

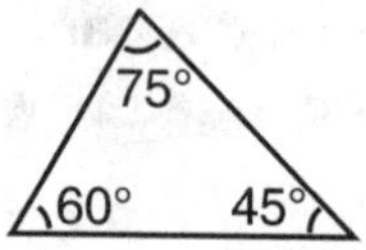

A. What is the sum of the angle measures of a triangle? ______ degrees

B. Why can't a triangle have two right angles?

____

____

____

Name/Date ____________________

Angle Measures of Triangles 2

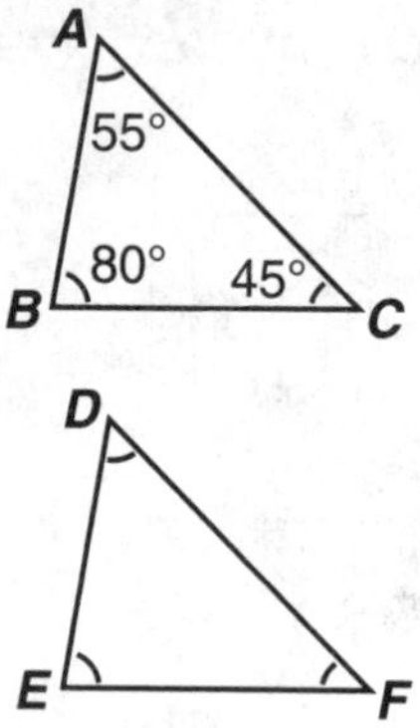

Triangle *ABC* is congruent to Triangle *DEF*.

A. Which angle is congruent to ∠*A*? ______

B. What is the measure of ∠*E*? ______

C. What is the measure of ∠*F*? ______

Name/Date ____________________

Angle Measures of Triangles 3

Write the missing angle measures.

A. ______

B. ______

C. ______

D. ______

A. 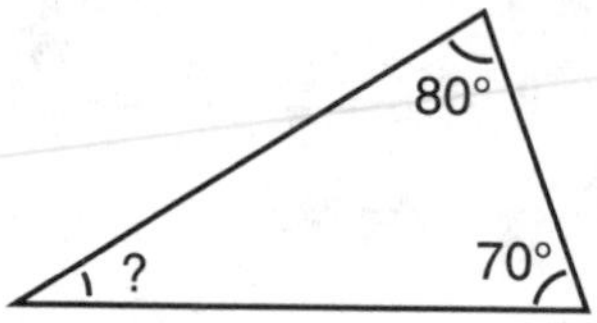

B. 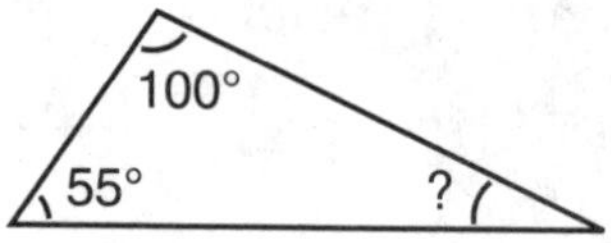

C. 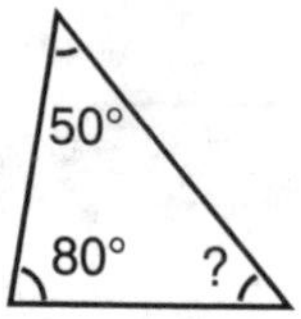

D. 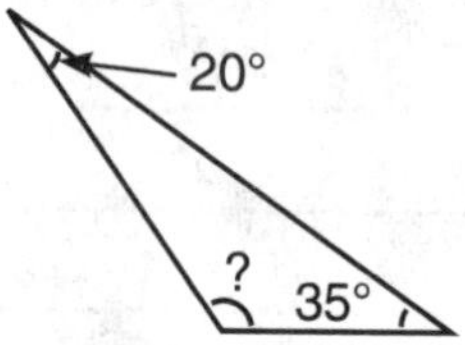

Name/Date ____________________

Angle Measures of Triangles 4

The triangles below are right triangles. Write the missing angle measures.

A. ______ 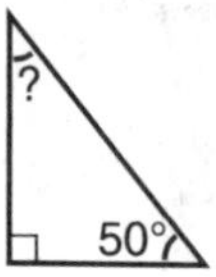

B. ______ 

C. ______ 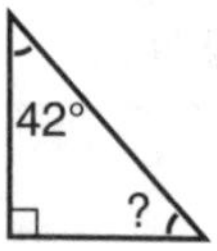

D. ______ 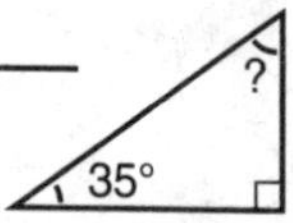

Name/Date ____________________

Angle Measures of Triangles 5

A. In a right triangle, the two acute angles have the same measure. What is their measure? ______

B. In an equilateral triangle, all the angles have the same measure. What is it? ______

C. In a right triangle, one acute angle is twice the size of the other. What are their measures? ______

Geometry Warm-ups: Angle Measures of Quadrilaterals

Name/Date ____________________

Angle Measures of Quadrilaterals 1

A. What is the sum of the angle measures of a quadrilateral?

_______ degrees

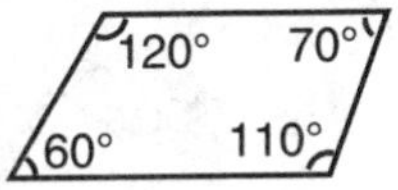

B. Why can't a quadrilateral have more than three obtuse angles?

____

____

____

Name/Date ____________________

Angle Measures of Quadrilaterals 2

The opposite angles of a parallelogram are congruent.

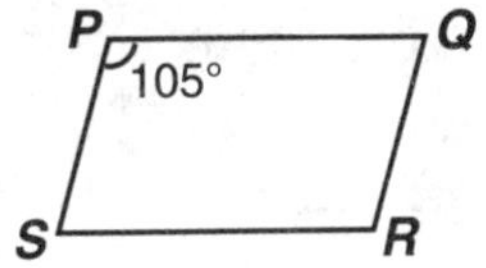

A. Which angle is congruent to $\angle P$? _______

B. What is the measure of $\angle Q$? _______

C. What is the sum of the measures of $\angle P$ and $\angle Q$? _______

Name/Date ____________________

Angle Measures of Quadrilaterals 3

Write the missing angle measures for each quadrilateral.

A. _______

B. _______

C. _______

D. _______

A.

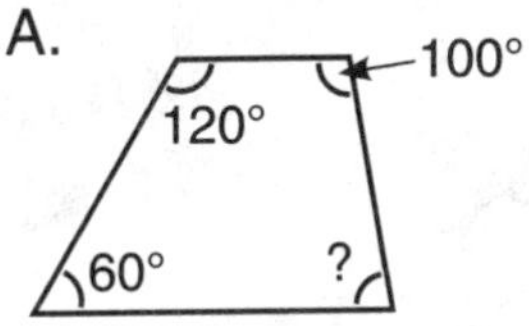

B.

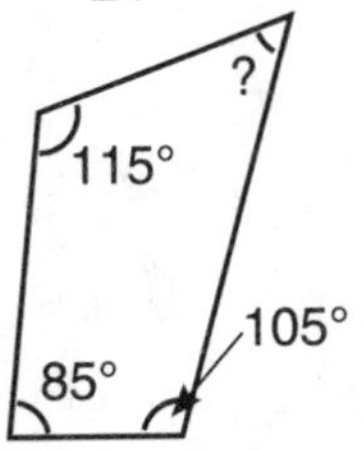

C.

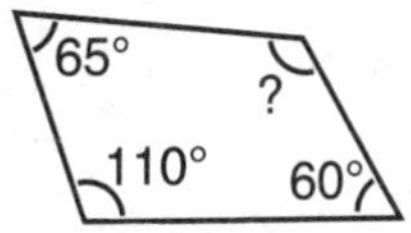

D.

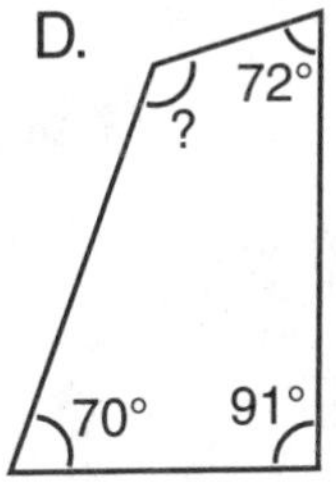

Name/Date ____________________

Angle Measures of Quadrilaterals 4

Write the missing angle measures for each quadrilateral.

A. _______

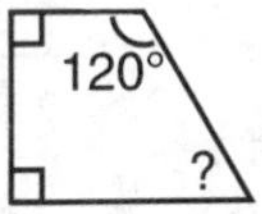

B. _______

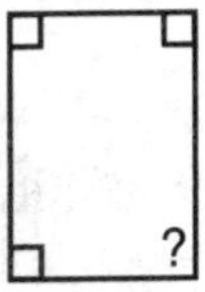

C. _______

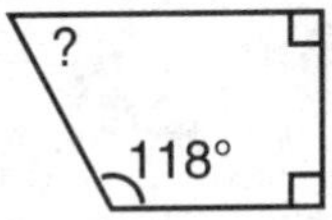

D. _______

Name/Date ____________________

Angle Measures of Quadrilaterals 5

This figure is a parallelogram. The measure of $\angle B$ is twice the measure of $\angle A$. What are the measures of the four angles?

$\angle A$ = _______°

$\angle B$ = _______°

$\angle C$ = _______°

$\angle D$ = _______°

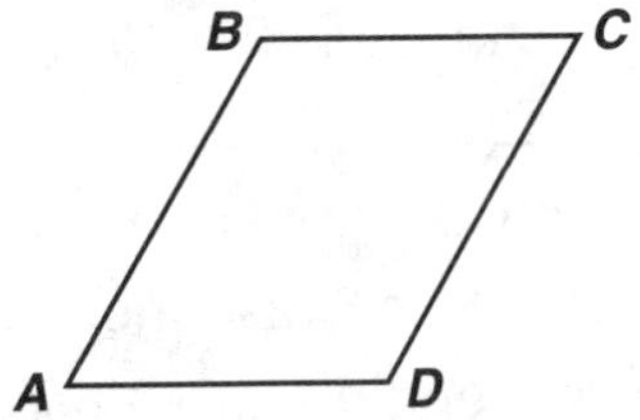

© Mark Twain Media, Inc., Publishers

Geometry Warm-ups: Perimeter of Rectangles and Squares

Name/Date ______________________________

Perimeter of Rectangles and Squares 1

Find the perimeter of each figure.

A. _______ m B. _______ in. C. _______ ft.

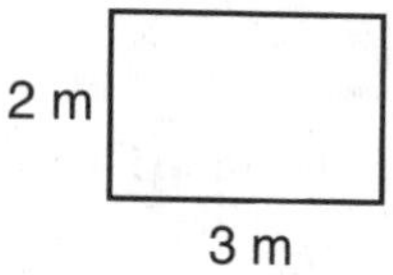

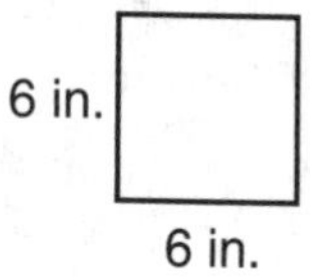

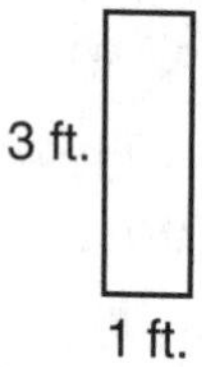

Name/Date ______________________________

Perimeter of Rectangles and Squares 2

A. A square has sides that are 7 feet long. What is its perimeter? ______________

B. A rectangle is 12 inches long and 10 inches wide. What is its perimeter? ______________

C. A rectangle is twice as long as it is wide. The rectangle is 8 meters wide. What is its perimeter? ______________

Name/Date ______________________________

Perimeter of Rectangles and Squares 3

A rectangle has a perimeter of 14 inches. The length of each side is a whole number in inches. Draw the possible rectangles with their measurements labeled.

Name/Date ______________________________

Perimeter of Rectangles and Squares 4

A. The perimeter of a square is 12 cm. What is the length of each side? ______________

B. The perimeter of a rectangle is 24 ft. The rectangle is 8 ft. long. What is its width?

____

C. The perimeter of a rectangle is 32 m. Its length is 6 m longer than its width. What are the length and width? ______________

Name/Date ______________________________

Perimeter of Rectangles and Squares 5

A. A square has sides that are 6 ft. long. What is its perimeter in feet? What is it in yards? __________

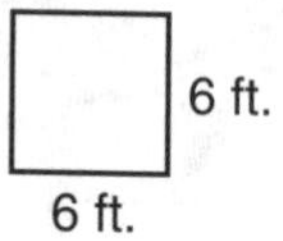

B. A rectangle is 24 in. x 48 in. What is its perimeter in inches? What is it in feet? ______________

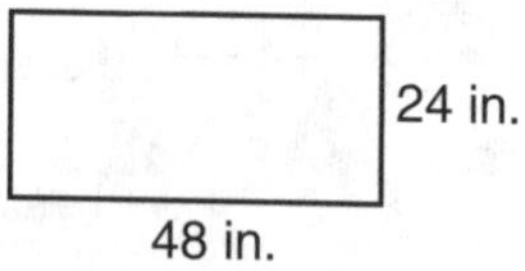

© Mark Twain Media, Inc., Publishers

Geometry Warm-ups: Perimeter of Polygons

Name/Date ____________________

Perimeter of Polygons 1

Find the perimeter of each triangle.

A.

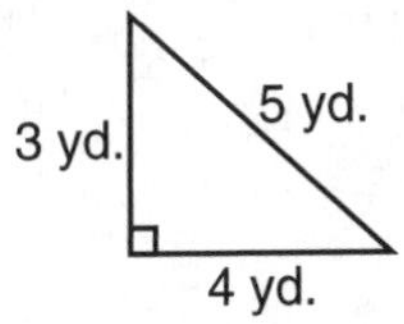

B.

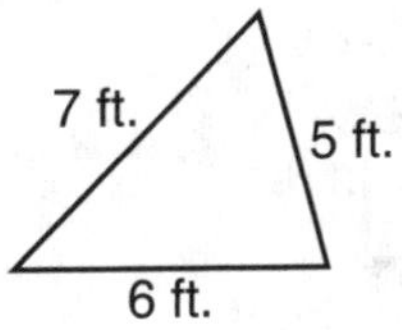

C.

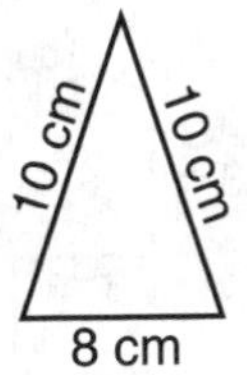

______ yd. ______ ft. ______ cm

Name/Date ____________________

Perimeter of Polygons 2

A regular polygon has sides of equal lengths. Find the perimeter of each regular polygon below.

A.

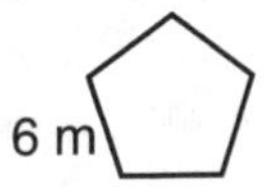

B.

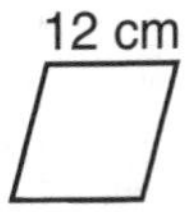

C.

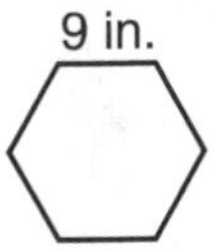

______ m ______ cm ______ in.

Name/Date ____________________

Perimeter of Polygons 3

Find the perimeter of each figure in both inches and feet.

A.

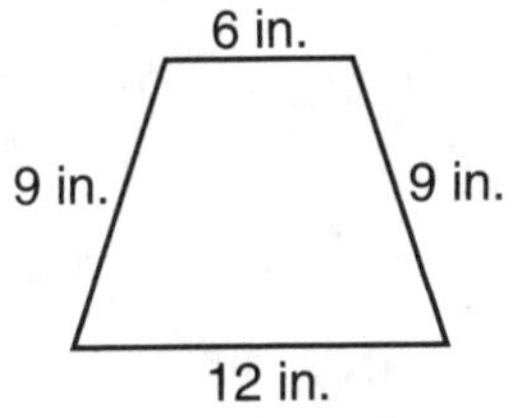

Perimeter = ______ in.
Perimeter = ______ ft.

B.

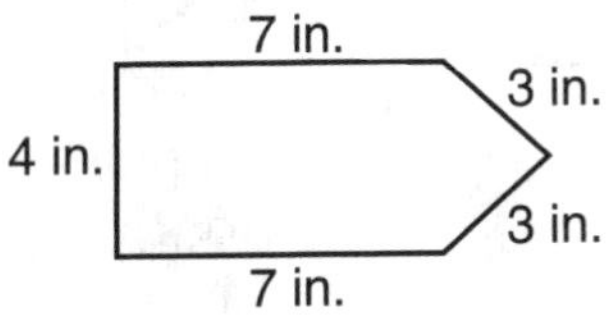

Perimeter = ______ in.
Perimeter = ______ ft.

C.

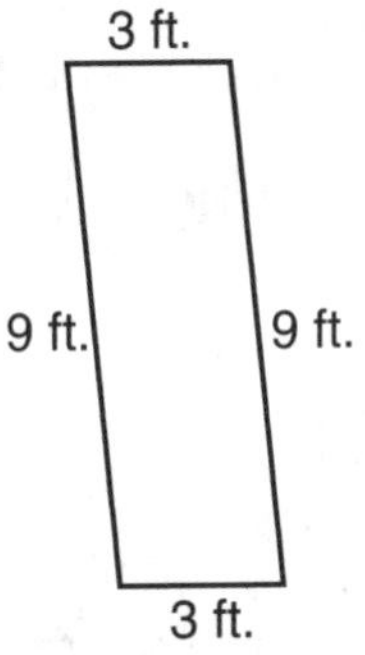

Perimeter = ______ in.
Perimeter = ______ ft.

Name/Date ____________________

Perimeter of Polygons 4

A. An equilateral triangle has a perimeter of 18 cm. What is the length of each side?

____

B. A regular pentagon has a perimeter of 45 ft. What is the length of each side? ______________

C. A rhombus has a perimeter of 28 m. What is the length of each side? ______________

Name/Date ____________________

Perimeter of Polygons 5

The figures are regular polygons. Write their number(s) to answer the questions.

A. Which figure has the greatest perimeter? ______

B. Which figure has the least perimeter? ______

C. Which figures have the same perimeter? ______

1.

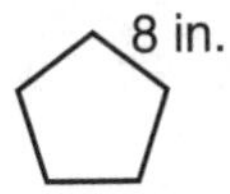

2.

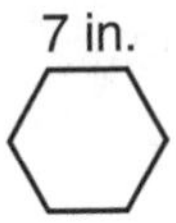

3.

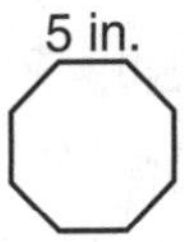

4.

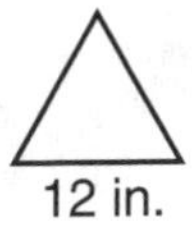

© Mark Twain Media, Inc., Publishers

Geometry Warm-ups: Perimeter of Complex Figures

Name/Date ____________________

Perimeter of Complex Figures 1

Find the perimeter of each figure.

A. ________ yd.

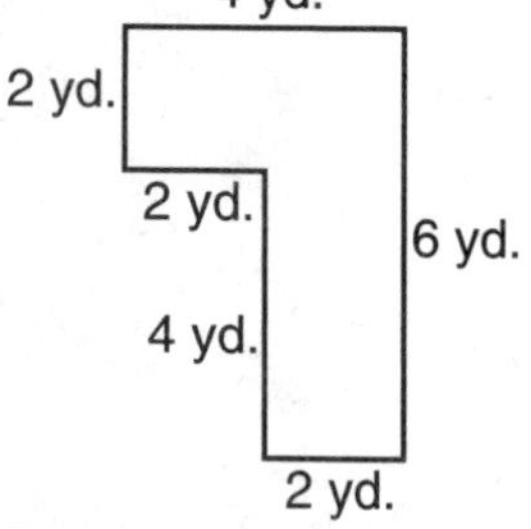

B. ________ cm

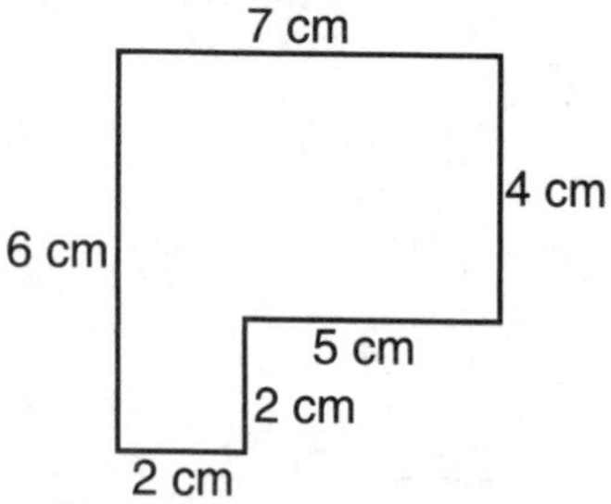

Name/Date ____________________

Perimeter of Complex Figures 2

Find the perimeter of each figure.

A. ________ m

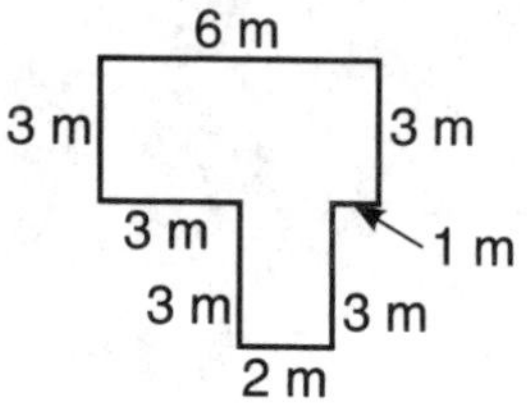

B. ________ in.

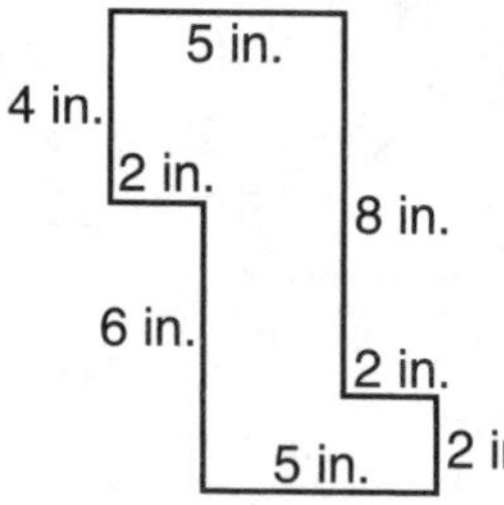

Name/Date ____________________

Perimeter of Complex Figures 3

Find the missing measures. Then find the perimeter.

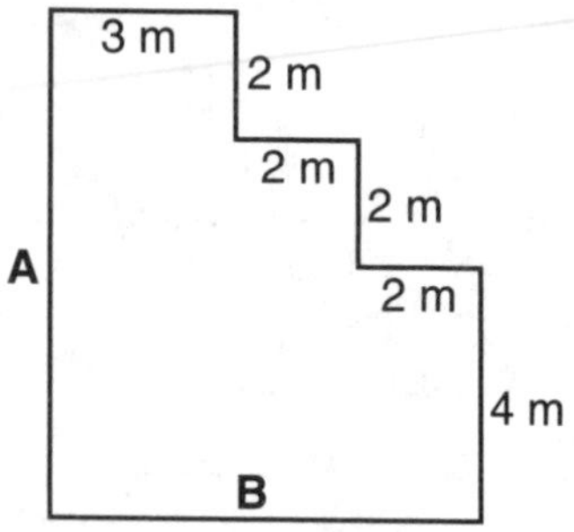

A = ________ m

B = ________ m

Perimeter =

________ m

Name/Date ____________________

Perimeter of Complex Figures 4

The diagram shows the shape of Lee's garden. Lee will put a fence around the garden. Fencing costs $2.00 per foot.

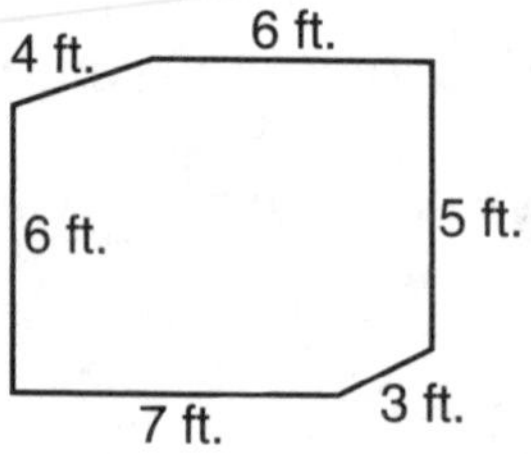

A. How many feet of fencing will Lee need?

____

B. How much will the fencing cost? ________

Name/Date ____________________

Perimeter of Complex Figures 5

Find the missing measures. Then find the perimeter of each figure.

A = ________ m Perimeter = ________ m

B = ________ in. Perimeter = ________ in.

C = ________ ft. Perimeter = ________ ft.

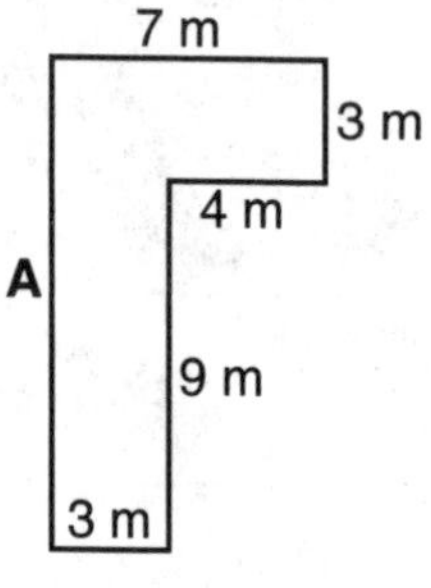

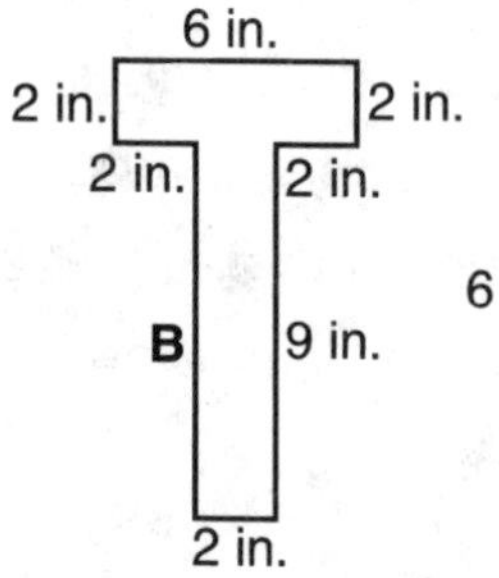

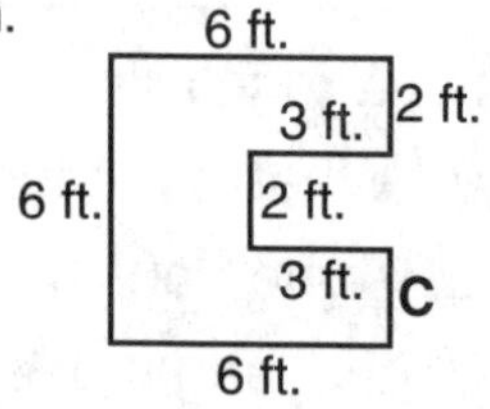

Geometry Warm-ups: Area of Rectangles and Squares

Name/Date ____________

Area of Rectangles and Squares 1

Find the area of each figure.

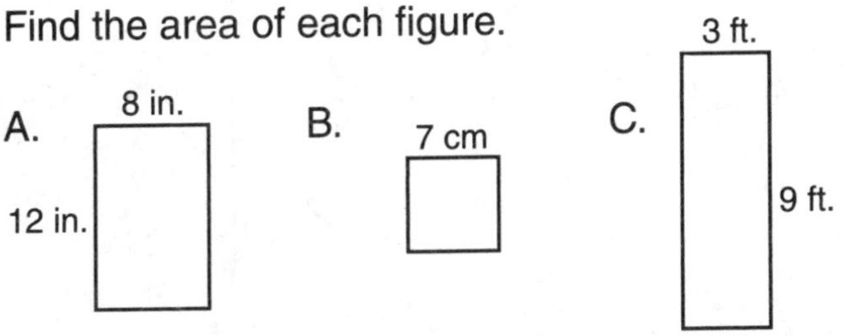

______ in.^{2} ______ cm^2 ______ ft.^{2}

Name/Date ____________

Area of Rectangles and Squares 2

A. Anna is getting a new carpet for her room. The floor is 12 feet wide and 15 feet long. How many square feet of carpeting will she need? ____________

B. The area of a rectangular rug is 760 square inches. The width of the rug is 20 inches. What is its length?

____

Name/Date ____________

Area of Rectangles and Squares 3

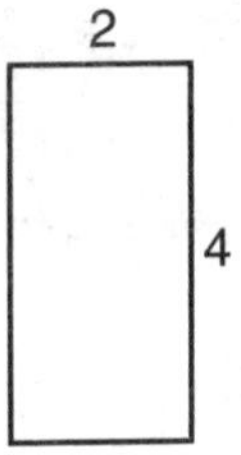

This rectangle has a perimeter of 12 units. Draw two other rectangles with a perimeter of 12 units. (Use only whole numbers for the lengths of the sides.)

Which of the rectangles has the greatest area? ____________

Name/Date ____________

Area of Rectangles and Squares 4

A. The side of a square measures 6 inches. What is the area of the square? ____________

B. The area of a square is 121 square centimeters. What is the length of each side? ____________

C. The area of a square is 9 square feet. What is its area measured in square yards?

____

Name/Date ____________

Area of Rectangles and Squares 5

A. A rectangle has a perimeter of 24 meters and an area of 32 square meters. What are the lengths of its sides?

____

B. The perimeter of a square is 28 inches. What is its area? ____________

© Mark Twain Media, Inc., Publishers

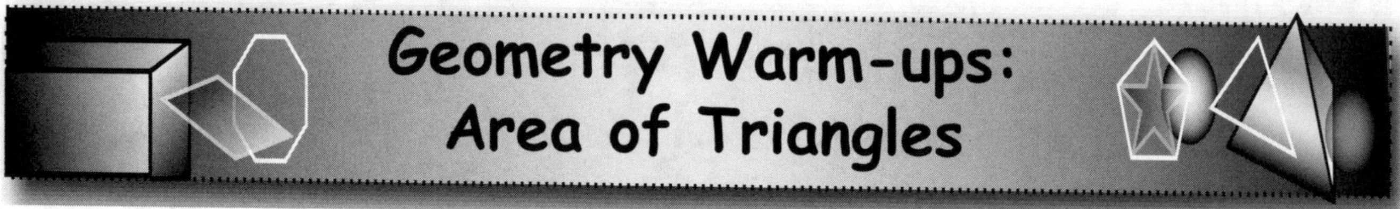

Geometry Warm-ups: Area of Triangles

Name/Date ______________________

Area of Triangles 1

Find the area of each triangle.

A. __________

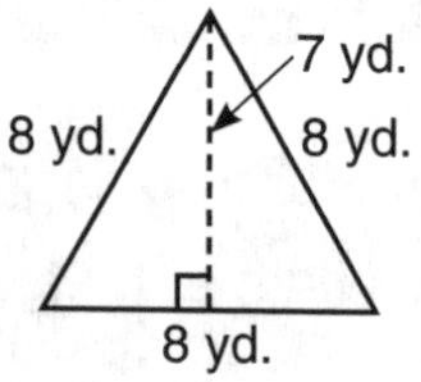

B. __________

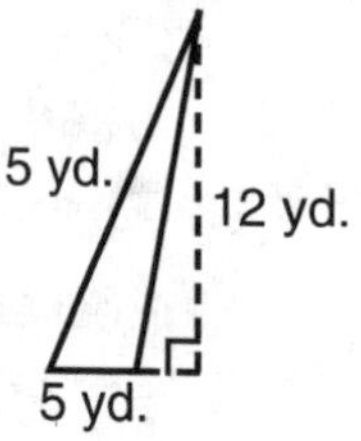

C. __________

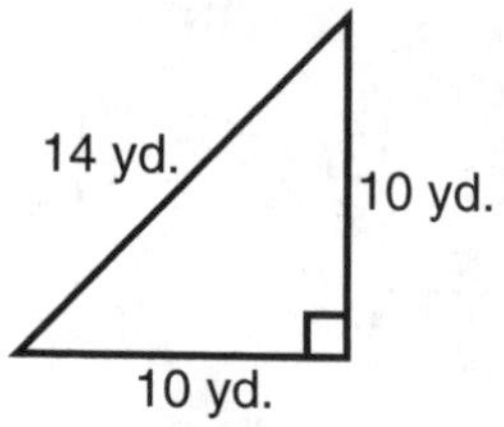

D. Which triangle has the greatest area—A, B, or C? ________

Name/Date ______________________

Area of Triangles 2

Find the area of each triangle.

A.

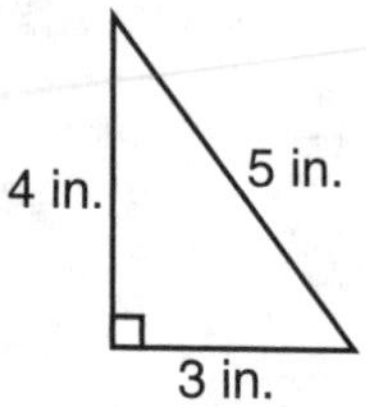

B.

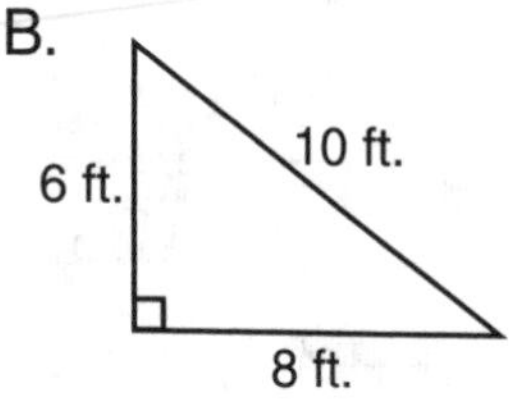

______ in.^2 ______ ft.^2

Name/Date ______________________

Area of Triangles 3

Find the area of each triangle.

A.

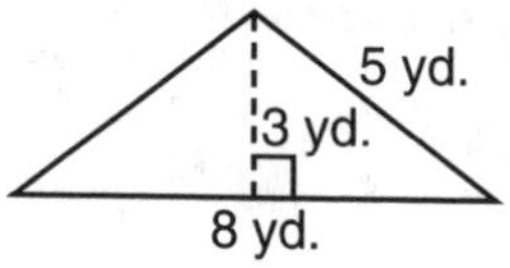

B.

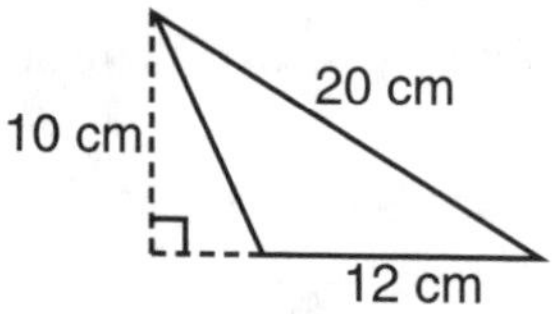

______ yd.^2 ______ cm^2

Name/Date ______________________

Area of Triangles 4

The area of this triangle can be expressed as $\frac{1}{2}ba$. Write an expression for the areas below.

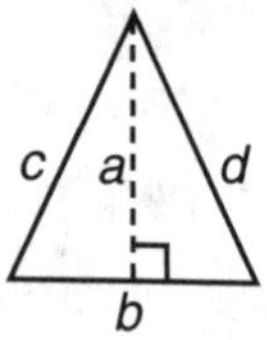

A.

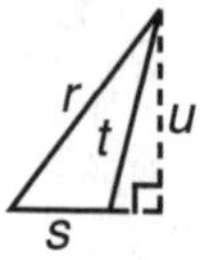

B.

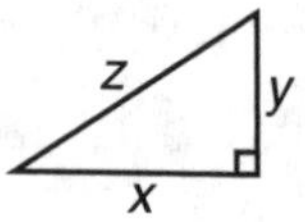

__________ __________

Name/Date ______________________

Area of Triangles 5

A. The area of a triangle is 60 cm^2. If the height is 15 cm, what is the length of the base?

____

B. The area of a triangle is 54 ft.^2. If the base is 9 ft., what is the height of the triangle? __________

© Mark Twain Media, Inc., Publishers

Geometry Warm-ups: Area of Parallelograms

Name/Date ____________

Area of Parallelograms 1

Find the area.

A. ________ ft.^{2}

B. ________ m^2

C. ________ yd.^{2}

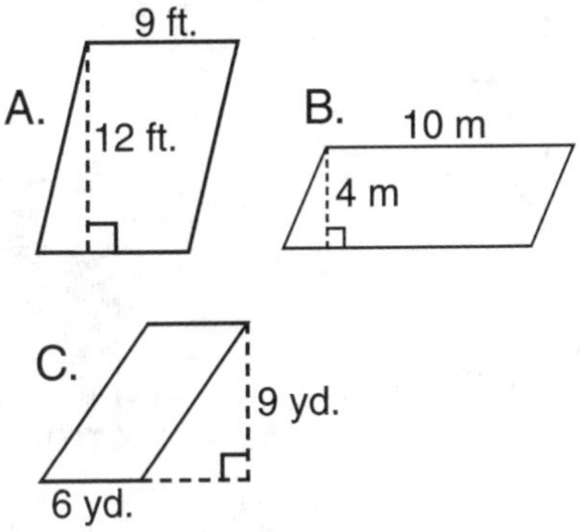

Name/Date ____________

Area of Parallelograms 2

Find the area.

A. ________ m^2 B. ________ cm^2

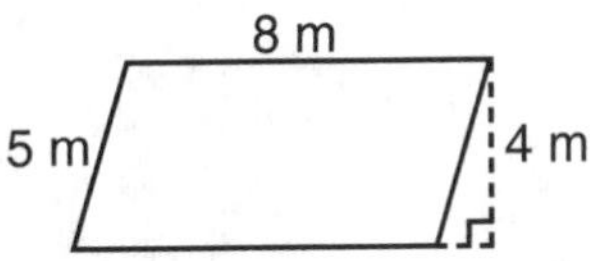

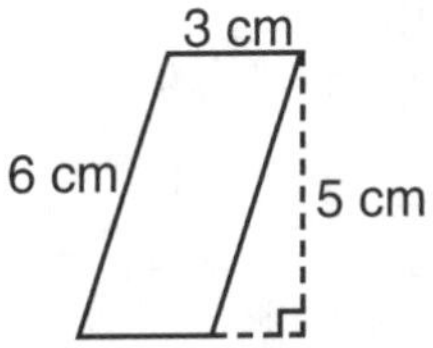

Name/Date ____________

Area of Parallelograms 3

Find the area.

A. ________ m^2

B. ________ m^2

C. ________ m^2

A.

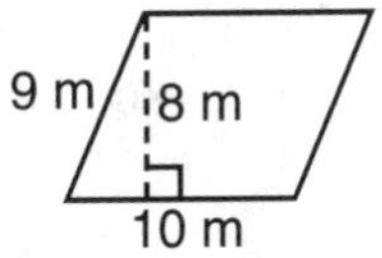

B.

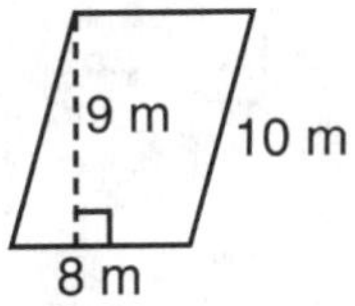

C.

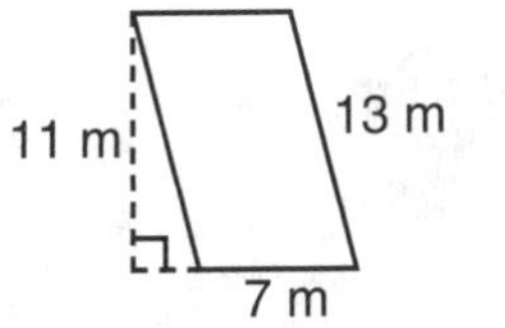

D. Which parallelogram has the greatest area? ________

E. Which one has the least area? ________

Name/Date ____________

Area of Parallelograms 4

A. A parallelogram has an area of 42 cm. It is 7 cm high. How long is the base? ________

B. A parallelogram has a base that is 12 in. long and a height of 7 in. What is its area? ________

C. A parallelogram has an area of 143 ft.^{2}. Its base is 11 ft. long. What is its height? ________

Name/Date ____________

Area of Parallelograms 5

A rhombus has a perimeter of 40 cm and a height of 8 cm.

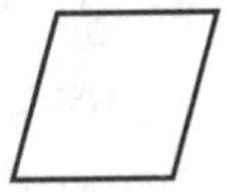

A. What is the length of each side? ________

B. What is the area of the rhombus? ________

(Hint: Draw a picture and label the sides to help you solve the problem.)

© Mark Twain Media, Inc., Publishers

Geometry Warm-ups: Area of Complex Figures

Name/Date ________________________________

Area of Complex Figures 1

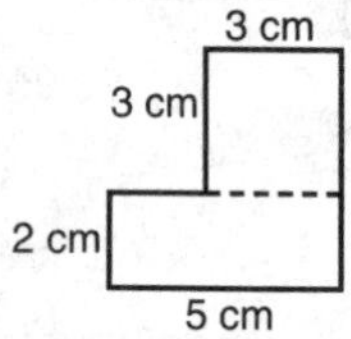

Area $= (3 \times 3) + (2 \times 5)$
$= 9 + 10$
$= 19\ \text{cm}^2$

Draw a line to divide each complex figure into two simple figures. Then find the area of the complex figure.

A.

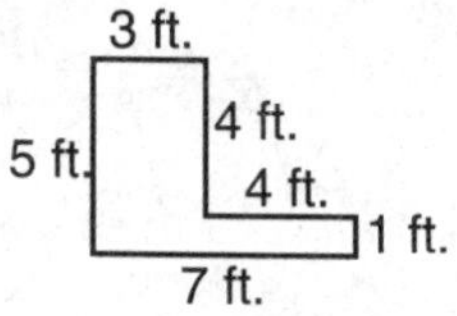

B.

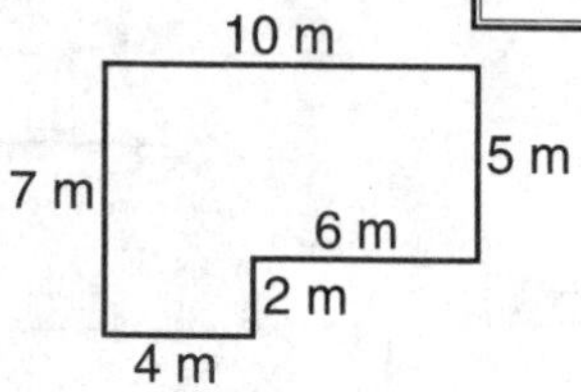

C.

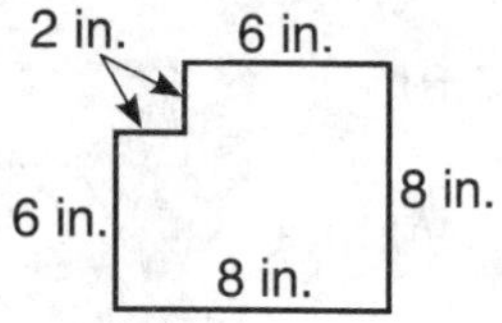

A. ________ ft.^2 B. ________ m^2 C. ________ in.^2

Name/Date ________________________________

Area of Complex Figures 2

Find the area of the figure.

Area = ________ m^2

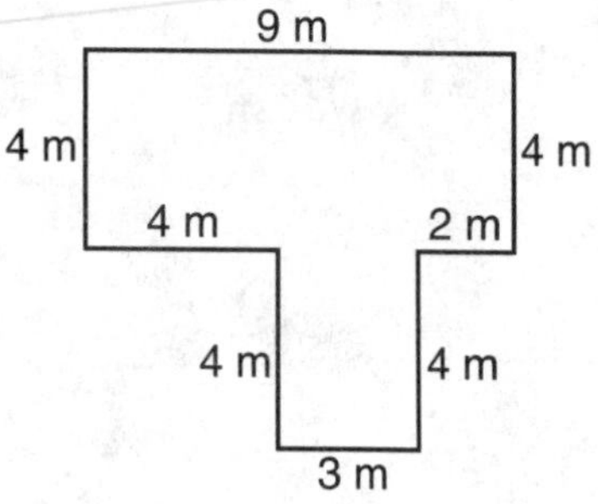

Name/Date ________________________________

Area of Complex Figures 3

Find the value of *x* and *y*. Then find the area of the figure.

x = ________ ft.

y = ________ ft.

Area = ________ ft.^2

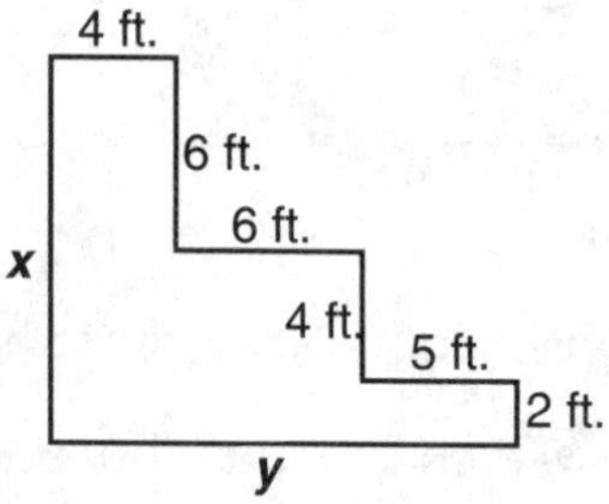

Name/Date ________________________________

Area of Complex Figures 4

Find the value of *x* and *y*. Then find the perimeter and area of the figure.

x = ________ yd.

y = ________ yd.

P = ________ yd.

A = ________ yd.^2

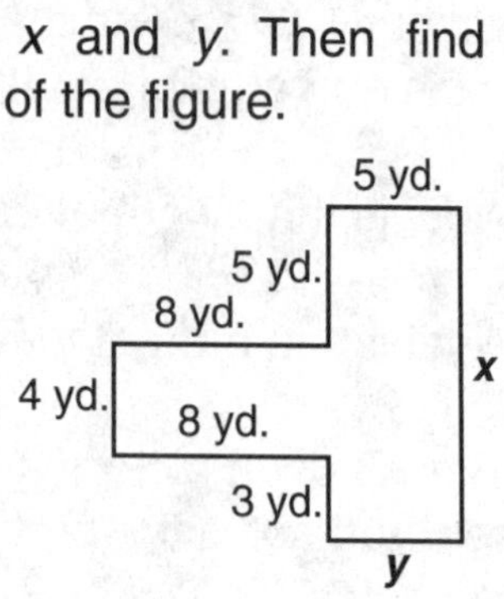

Name/Date ________________________________

Area of Complex Figures 5

Find the value of *x* and *y*. Then find the perimeter and area of the figure.

x = ________ in.

y = ________ in.

P = ________ in.

A = ________ in.^2

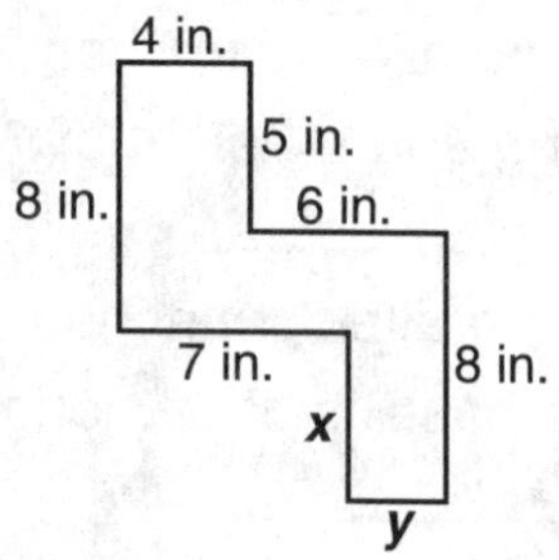

Geometry Warm-ups: Area of Irregular Regions

Name/Date ______________________________

Area of Irregular Regions 1

Estimate the area of each irregular region in square units. First count each whole square that is covered. Then count each partial square as half a square. Add that amount to the number of whole squares.

This shape covers 2 whole squares and 10 partial ones. The total area is 7 square units (2 whole squares and 10 half-squares).

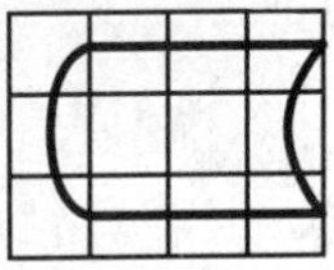

A.

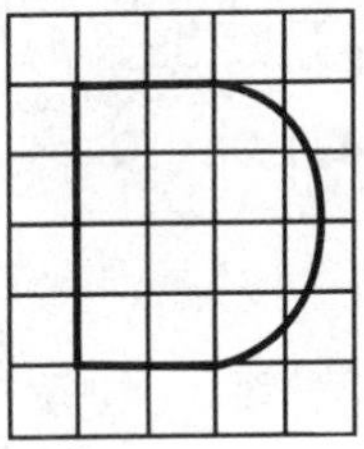

B.

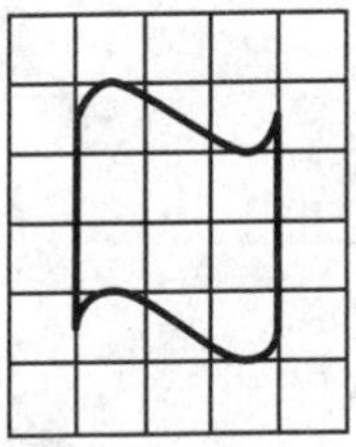

A. ________ square units

B. ________ square units

Name/Date ______________________________

Area of Irregular Regions 2

Estimate the number of square units in the region.

________ square units

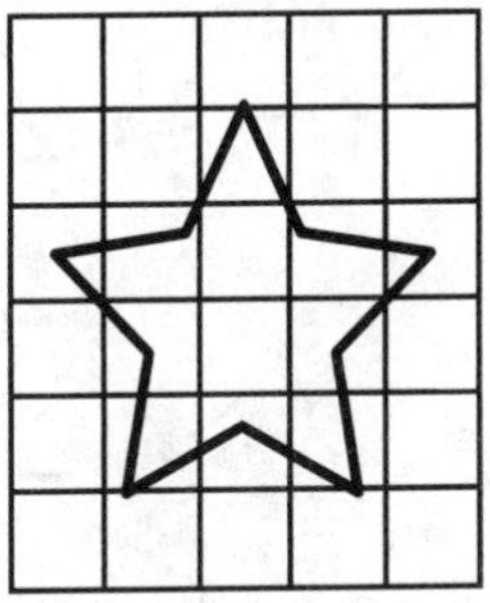

Name/Date ______________________________

Area of Irregular Regions 3

Estimate the number of square units in the region.

________ square units

Name/Date ______________________________

Area of Irregular Regions 4

Draw an irregular shape on the grid. Estimate its area.

A = ________

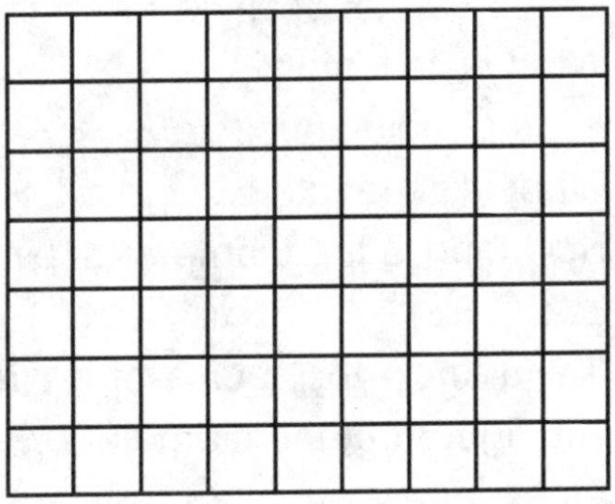

Name/Date ______________________________

Area of Irregular Regions 5

Trace your hand on a sheet of graph paper. Count the squares to determine its area.

Geometry Warm-ups: Circles

Name/Date ____________________

Circles 1

Write the word that matches each figure. Use the words in the box.

radius	**center**
diameter	**chord**

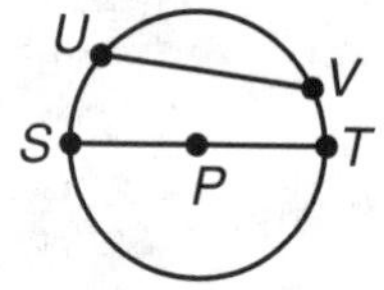

A. Point *P* __________ B. $\overline{PT}$ __________

C. $\overline{UV}$ __________ D. $\overline{ST}$ __________

Name/Date ____________________

Circles 2

Draw a circle that contains the following:

A. center *M*
B. diameter $\overline{NS}$
C. radius $\overline{MP}$
D. chord $\overline{ST}$

Name/Date ____________________

Circles 3

Name the following:

A. two diameters __________

B. center of the circle __________

C. one chord __________

D. four radii __________

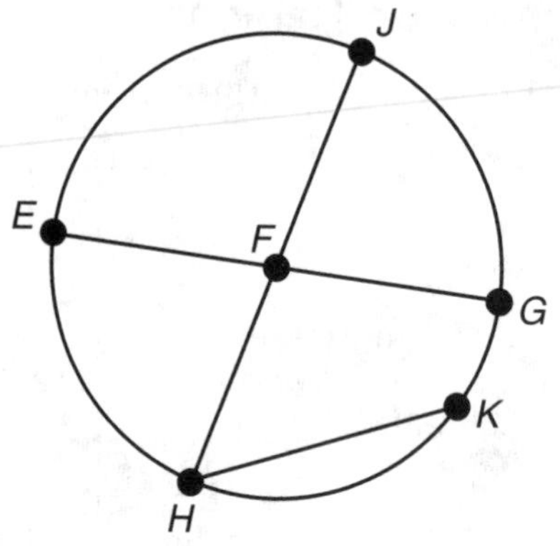

Name/Date ____________________

Circles 4

Write the correct word for each.

chord
diameter
radius
semicircle

A. Has one endpoint on a circle and the other endpoint at the center __________
B. Has both endpoints on a circle __________
C. Half a circle __________
D. Passes through the center of a circle and has both endpoints on the circle __________

Name/Date ____________________

Circles 5

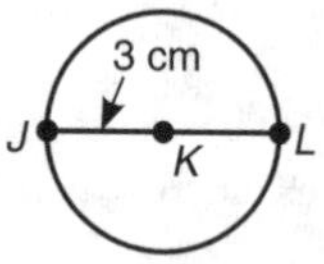

A. $\overline{JK}$ is a radius of circle *K*. What is its length? __________
B. $\overline{KL}$ is a radius of circle *K*. What is its length? __________
C. How long is the diameter of circle *K*? __________
D. If you know the radius of a circle, how can you figure out the diameter? __________

Geometry Warm-ups: Circles and Central Angles

Name/Date ____________________

Circles and Central Angles 1

A central angle is an angle that has its vertex at the center of a circle. ∠*ABC* is a central angle. List two other central angles.

____

____

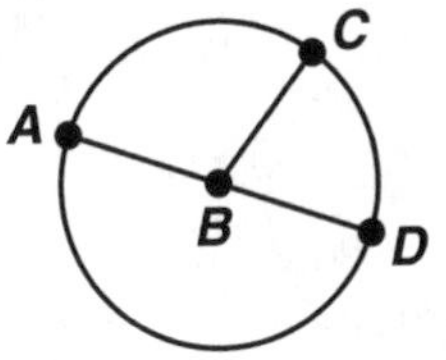

Name/Date ____________________

Circles and Central Angles 2

There are 360° in a circle.

A. What is the measure of ∠*PQR*? ______

B. What is the measure of ∠*PQS*? ______

C. What is the measure of ∠*SQR*? ______

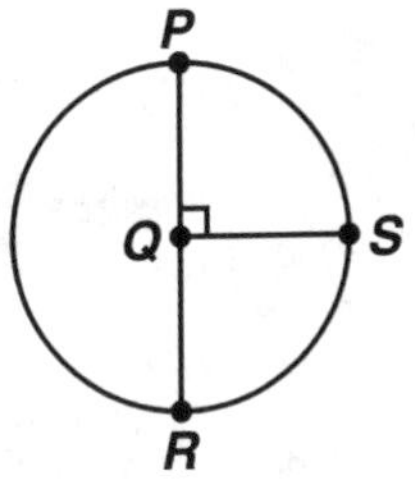

Name/Date ____________________

Circles and Central Angles 3

Write "**A**" if the statement is always true, "**S**" if it is sometimes true, and "**N**" if it is never true.

A. A central angle is greater than 90 degrees. ______

B. A central angle is formed by two radii of a circle. ______

C. A chord can be part of a central angle. ______

D. A diameter of a circle can form a central angle. ______

Name/Date ____________________

Circles and Central Angles 4

Draw the following features and label them on your diagram.

A. center *L*

B. radius $\overline{LM}$

C. chord $\overline{SM}$

D. central angle ∠*XLY*

E. central angle ∠*XLZ*

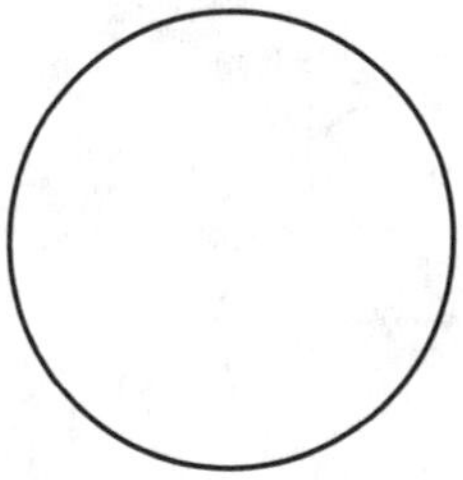

Name/Date ____________________

Circles and Central Angles 5

A. Draw two diameters on the first circle so that they form four central angles measuring 90°.

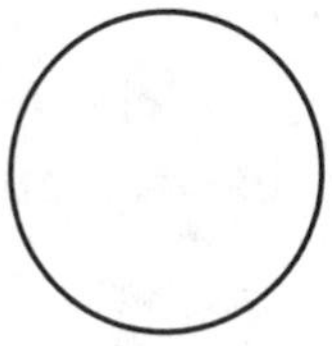

B. Draw two diameters on the second circle so that they form two obtuse central angles and two acute central angles.

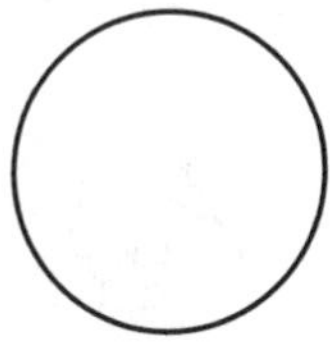

© Mark Twain Media, Inc., Publishers

Geometry Warm-ups: Circumference

Name/Date ____________________

Circumference 1

Fill in the blanks. You will not use all the answers provided.

area
perimeter
three
five
π x *d*
π x *r*

A. The circumference is the ____________ of a circle.

B. The circumference is about ____________ times greater than the diameter.

C. The formula for finding circumference is ____________.

Name/Date ____________________

Circumference 2

Find the circumference. Use $\frac{22}{7}$ for π .

A. ________ in.

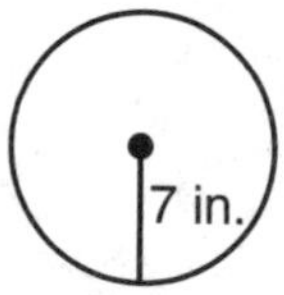

B. ________ yd.

Name/Date ____________________

Circumference 3

Find the circumference. Use 3.14 for π.

A. ________ cm

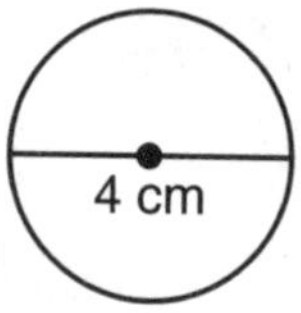

B. ________ m

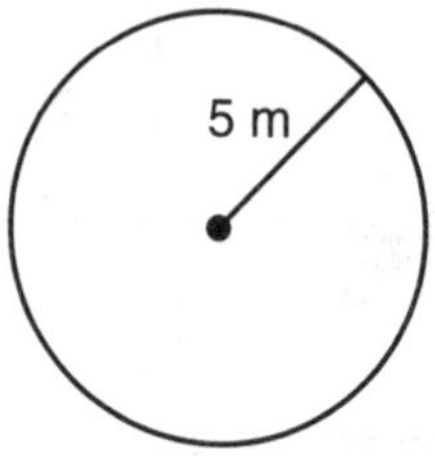

Name/Date ____________________

Circumference 4

Use 3.14 for π to solve the problems.

A. The diameter of a circle is 8 cm. What is the circumference? ____________

B. The radius of a circle is 2.5 ft. What is the circumference? ____________

C. The circumference of a circle is 28.26 in. What is the diameter? ____________

Name/Date ____________________

Circumference 5

Find the circumference. Use 3.14 for π and express the answer as a decimal. Or use $\frac{22}{7}$ for π and express the answer as a fraction in simplest form.

A. ____________

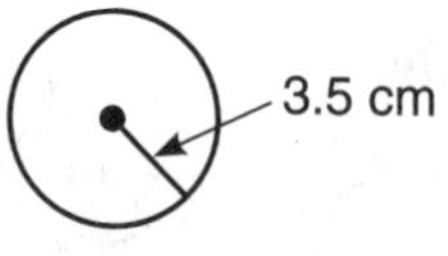

B. ____________

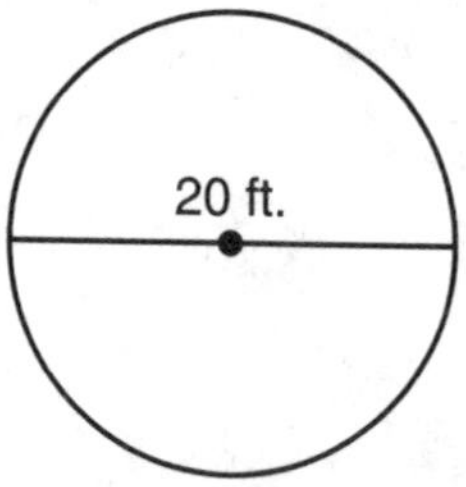

C. ____________

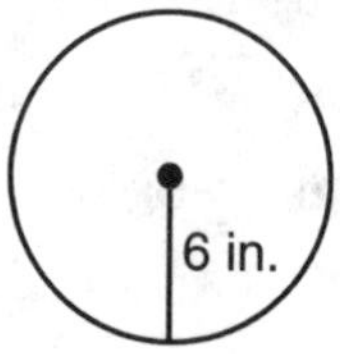

© Mark Twain Media, Inc., Publishers

Geometry Warm-ups: Area of Circles

Name/Date ______________________________

Area of Circles 1

The formula for finding the area of a circle with radius (r) is $\pi \times r \times r$, or πr^2.

Find each area. Use 3.14 for π.

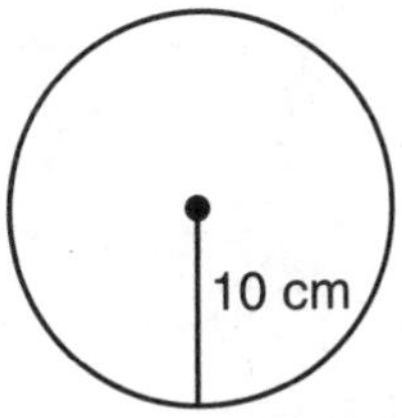

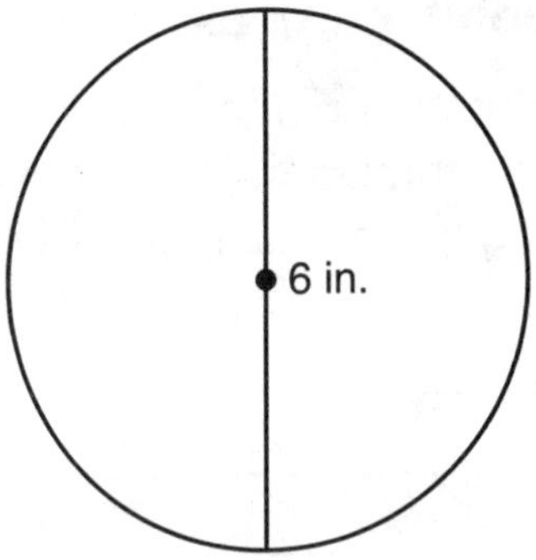

A. ________ cm^2 B. ________ $in.^2$

Name/Date ______________________________

Area of Circles 2

Find each area. Use $\frac{22}{7}$ for π. Express the answer as a fraction in simplest form.

A. ________ m^2 B. ________ $ft.^2$

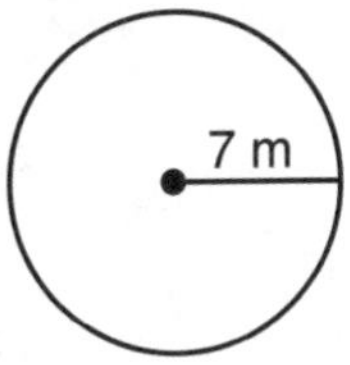

Name/Date ______________________________

Area of Circles 3

Use 3.14 for π to solve the problems.

A. The radius of a circle is 5 cm. What is the area? ________ cm^2

B. The diameter of a circle is 40 yd. What is the area? ________ $yd.^2$

Name/Date ______________________________

Area of Circles 4

The circumference of a circle is 62.8 m.

A. How can you find the area? ______________________________

____

____

____

B. Find the area. ______________

Name/Date ______________________________

Area of Circles 5

Find an object that is shaped like a circle. For example, you can use the base of a can or the lid of a jar. Estimate the area. Then, measure the diameter or radius with a ruler and calculate.

My object: ______________________________

My estimate of area: ______________________________

My calculations: ______________________________

© Mark Twain Media, Inc., Publishers

Geometry Warm-ups: Solid Figures

Name/Date ______________________

Solid Figures 1

Write the name of each figure.
Use the words in the box.
You will not use all the words.

cube	**cone**	**triangular prism**	**triangular pyramid**
square pyramid	**rectangular prism**	**sphere**	**cylinder**

A. ______________________
B. ______________________
C. ______________________
D. ______________________

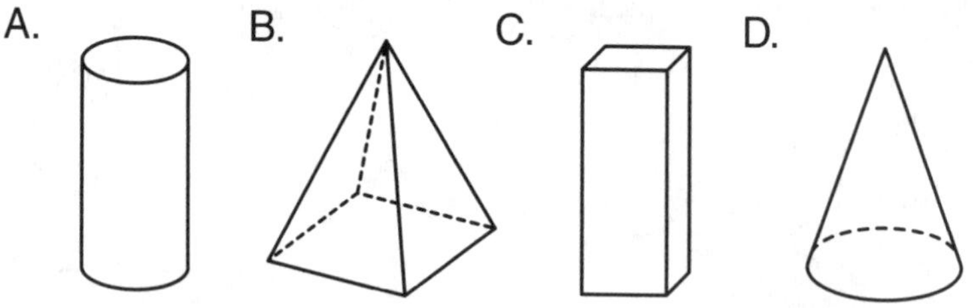

Name/Date ______________________

Solid Figures 2

A. Can a pyramid have a triangle for a base? ________

B. Can a pyramid have a square for a base? ________

C. Does a cylinder have any vertices? ______

D. Does a cone have any vertices? ______

E. Is a cube a rectangular prism?______

Name/Date ______________________

Solid Figures 3

Write the number of faces, or flat surfaces, each figure has.

A. cube ______

B. cone ______

C. rectangular prism ______

D. square pyramid ______

E. cylinder ______

Name/Date ______________________

Solid Figures 4

Complete the table.

	Figure	Number of Edges	Number of Vertices
A.	Cube	12	
B.	Square Pyramid		
C.	Triangular Pyramid		
D.	Rectangular Prism		

Name/Date ______________________

Solid Figures 5

Are the statements true? Write **"A"** for always, **"S"** for sometimes, or **"N"** for never.

A. A pyramid has a square base. ______

B. The faces of a cube are congruent. ______

C. A cylinder has two circular faces that are congruent. ______

D. A sphere has a circular face. ______

© Mark Twain Media, Inc., Publishers

Geometry Warm-ups: Solid Figures and Nets

Name/Date ______________________________

Solid Figures and Nets 1

A net is a flat pattern that can be folded to make a solid figure. Write the name of the solid below its net. Use the words in the box. (You will not use all the words.)

cube	**cone**	**triangular prism**
triangular pyramid		**square pyramid**
rectangular prism		

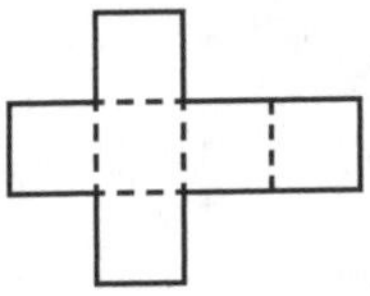

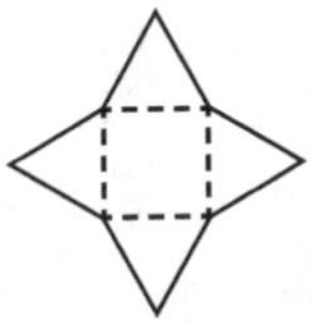

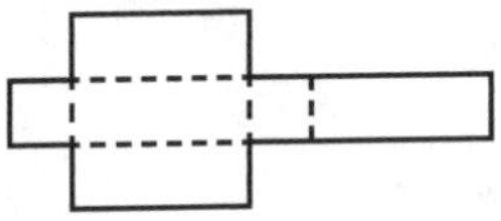

A. ______________ B. ______________ C. ______________

Name/Date ______________________________

Solid Figures and Nets 2

Draw dashed lines to complete the nets.

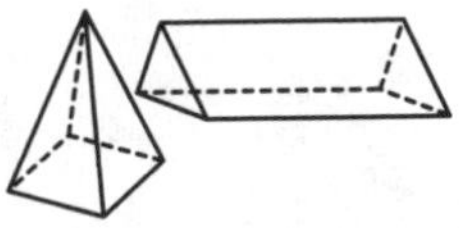

A. triangular prism

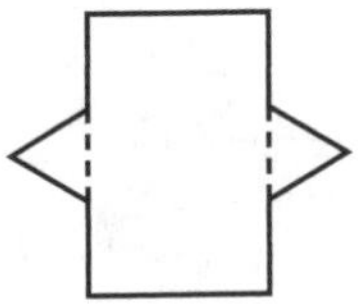

B. square pyramid

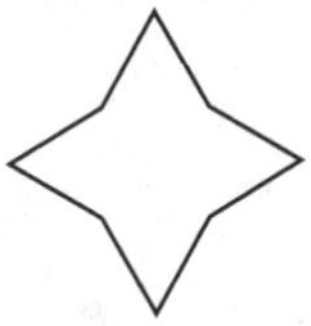

Name/Date ______________________________

Solid Figures and Nets 3

A cube can have different nets. Draw two of the possible nets in the space below.

Name/Date ______________________________

Solid Figures and Nets 4

A. A cube is a special rectangular prism. How is its net similar to nets of all rectangular prisms? ______________________________

____

B. How is a cube's net different from that of another rectangular prism? ______________________________

____

____

Name/Date ______________________________

Solid Figures and Nets 5

A triangular pyramid has four triangular faces. Which diagram shows a net of a triangular pyramid? ______

A.

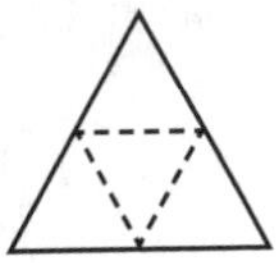

B.

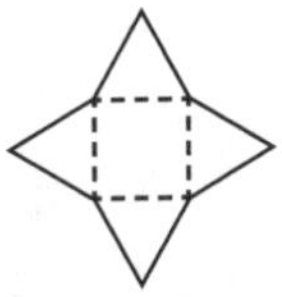

Check your answer by first copying the patterns onto paper. Then cut them out and fold them.

© Mark Twain Media, Inc., Publishers

Geometry Warm-ups: Surface Area of Rectangular Prisms

Name/Date ______________________________

Surface Area of Rectangular Prisms 1

Use the net to find the surface area of the cube.

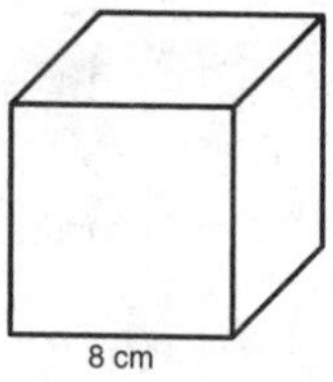

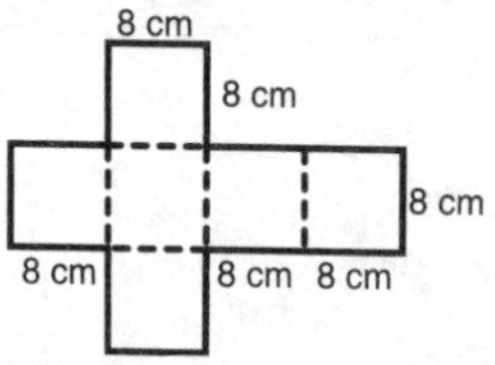

Surface Area = ________ cm^2

Name/Date ______________________________

Surface Area of Rectangular Prisms 2

Use the net to find the surface area of the rectangular prism.

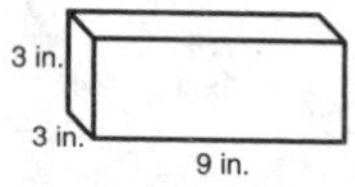

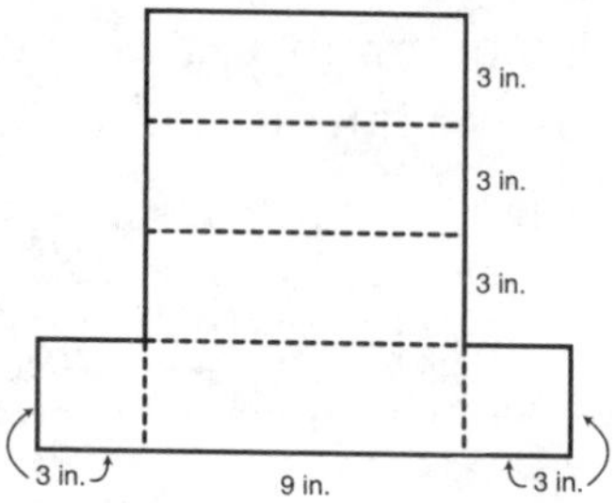

Surface Area = ________ $in.^2$

Name/Date ______________________________

Surface Area of Rectangular Prisms 3

Find the surface area of each figure.

A.

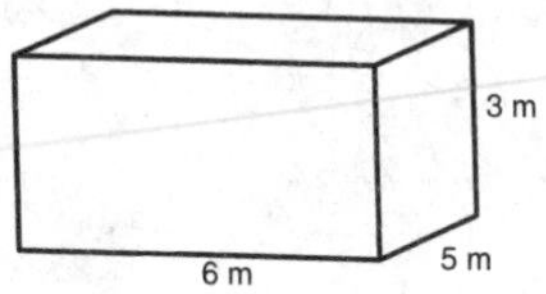

B.

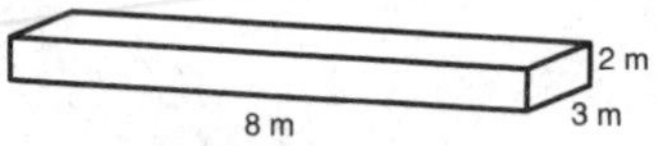

C.

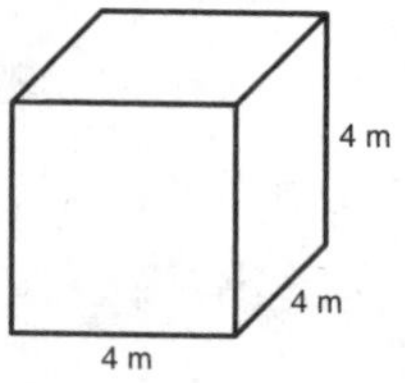

Surface Area = ________ m^2 Surface Area = ________ m^2 Surface Area = ________ m^2

D. Which block has the greatest surface area? ________

Name/Date ______________________________

Surface Area of Rectangular Prisms 4

A cube has sides measuring 5 inches. What is the surface area of the cube? ________

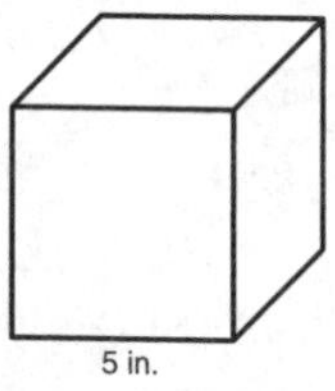

Name/Date ______________________________

Surface Area of Rectangular Prisms 5

Fill in the chart, and then answer the question.

What happens to the surface area when the sides of a cube are doubled?

Side of Cube	Surface Area
1	
2	
4	
8	

____

Geometry Warm-ups: Volume of Rectangular Prisms

Name/Date ____________________

Volume of Rectangular Prisms 1

Matt wants to fill this box with one-inch cubes. How many cubes will he need? ______ cubes

How did you find the answer?

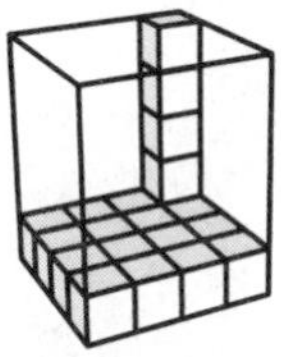

____

____

____

____

Name/Date ____________________

Volume of Rectangular Prisms 2

Find the volume of each cube.

A.

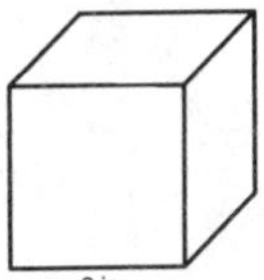

B.

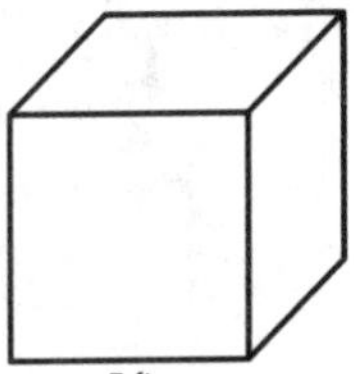

Volume = ______ in.^{3} Volume = ______ ft.^{3}

Name/Date ____________________

Volume of Rectangular Prisms 3

Find the volume.

A. Volume = ______ cm^3

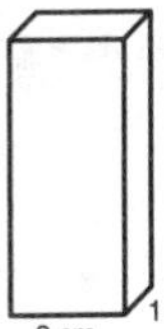

B. Volume = ______ m^3

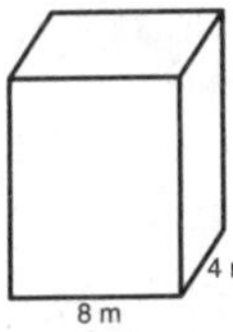

Name/Date ____________________

Volume of Rectangular Prisms 4

Kim wants to get the box with the greater volume. Which box should she get—A or B?

______

Box A:	Box B:
length = 6 in.	length = 8 in.
width = 7 in.	width = 6 in.
height = 5 in.	height = 4 in.
Volume = ______ in.^{3}	Volume = ______ in.^{3}

Name/Date ____________________

Volume of Rectangular Prisms 5

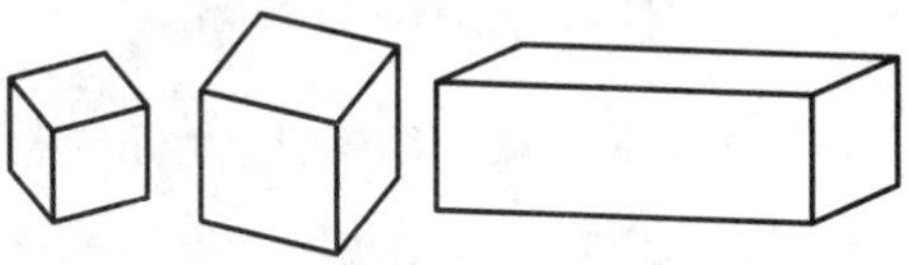

A. A cube has a volume of 216 cubic feet.

What is the length of each side? ____________________

B. The volume of a rectangular prism is 128 cm^3. The prism is 8 cm long and 4 cm high.

What is its width? ____________________

C. The surface area of a cube is 24 square inches. What is its volume? ____________________

Geometry Warm-ups: Volume of Cylinders

Name/Date ____________________

Volume of Cylinders 1

Find the volume of each cylinder. First find the area of the circular base (B). Then multiply that by the height to find the volume (V).

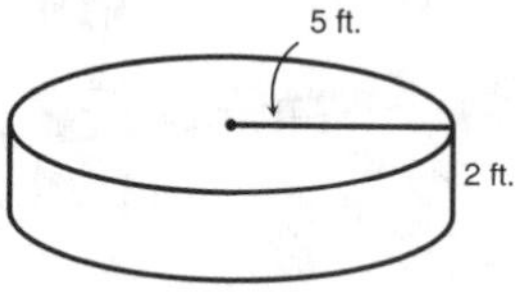

$B = \pi r^2$
$= 3.14 \times 5^2$
$= 78.5 \text{ ft.}^2$

$V = 78.5 \times 2$
$= 157 \text{ ft.}^3$

A.

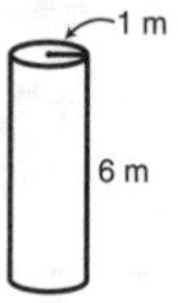

B = ________ m^2
V = ________ m^3

B.

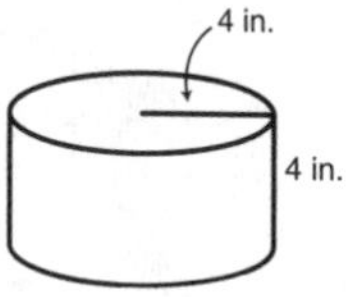

B = ________ $in.^2$
V = ________ $in.^3$

Name/Date ____________________

Volume of Cylinders 2

Fill in the blanks with words from the box.

area
cubic
circle
height

A. A cylinder's base is a ________.

B. To find the ________ of the cylinder's base, use the formula πr^2.

C. To find the volume of a cylinder, multiply the area of the base by the ________.

D. Volume is measured in ________ units.

Name/Date ____________________

Volume of Cylinders 3

Which figure has the greater volume—A or B? ______

A.

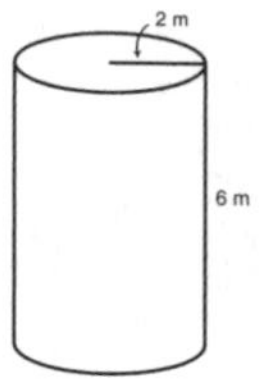

B = ________
V = ________

B.

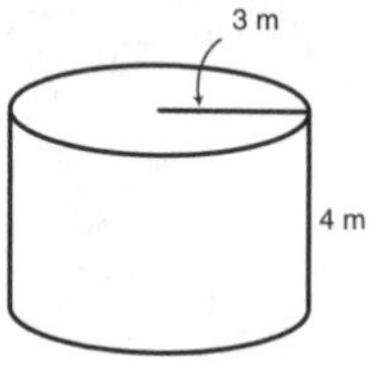

B = ________
V = ________

Name/Date ____________________

Volume of Cylinders 4

A. What is the volume of a cylinder that has a radius of 10 cm and a height of 10 cm?

____

B. What is the volume of a cylinder that has a radius of 5 cm and a height of 10 cm?

____

Name/Date ____________________

Volume of Cylinders 5

A. The volume of a cylinder is 141.3 $yd.^3$. The height of the cylinder is 5 yd. What is the area of the cylinder's base? ________

B. How did you solve the problem?

____
____
____

Geometry Warm-ups: Volume of Triangular Prisms

Name/Date ______________________________

Volume of Triangular Prisms 1

To find the volume of a triangular prism, first find the area of the triangular base (B). Then multiply that by the prism's height to find the volume (V).

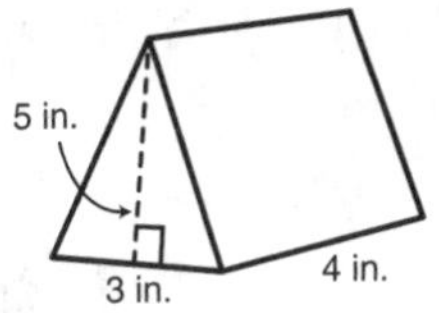

$B = \frac{1}{2} \times 3 \times 5$
$= 7.5 \text{ in.}^2$
$V = 7.5 \times 4$
$= 30 \text{ in.}^3$

A.

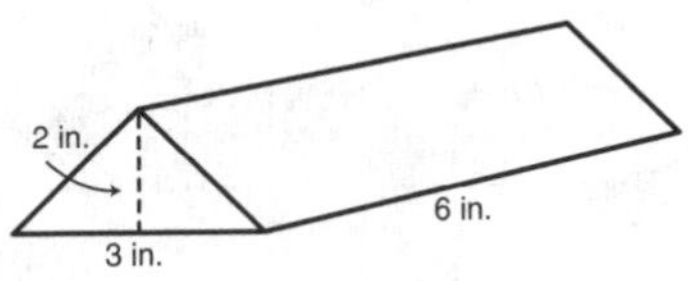

B = ________ in.^{2}

V = ________ in.^{3}

B.

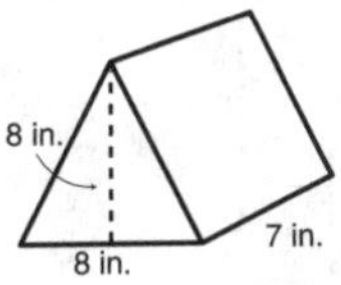

B = ________ m^2

V = ________ m^3

Name/Date ______________________________

Volume of Triangular Prisms 2

Circle the correct answer for each statement.

A. The base of a triangular prism is a (triangle / rectangle).

B. The area of a triangular base equals ($\frac{1}{2}$ / $\frac{1}{3}$) times the triangle's height times its base.

C. The volume of a triangular prism equals the area of the base of the prism times its (area / height).

Name/Date ______________________________

Volume of Triangular Prisms 3

First find the area of the base (B). Then find the volume (V) of the prism.

B = ______________

V = ______________

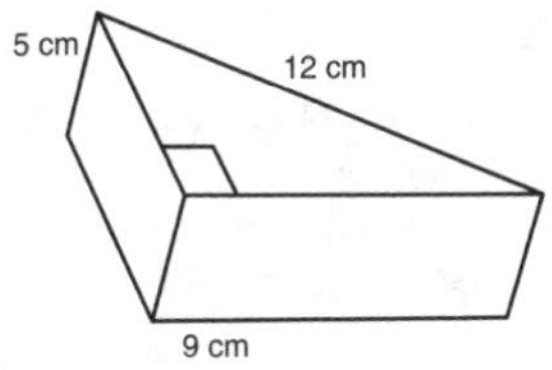

Name/Date ______________________________

Volume of Triangular Prisms 4

A. A triangular prism has a base whose area is 14 in.^{2}. Its height is 5 inches. What is the volume of the prism? ______________

B. A triangular prism has a volume of 54 cm^3. Its height is 3 cm. What is the area of the triangular base? ______________

Name/Date ______________________________

Volume of Triangular Prisms 5

Which has the greater volume—A or B? ________

A. V = ____________

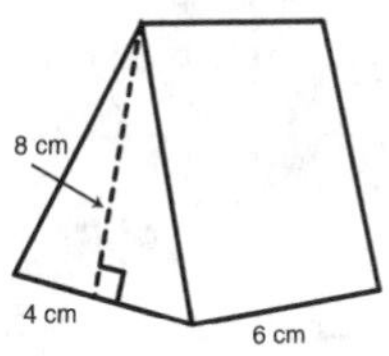

B. V = ____________

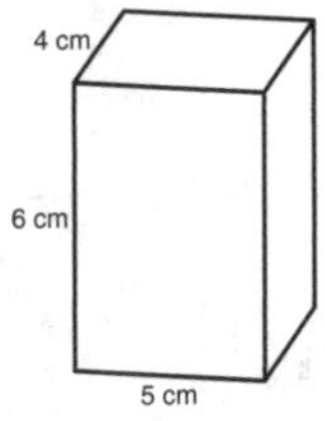

© Mark Twain Media, Inc., Publishers

Geometry Warm-ups: Ordered Pairs

Name/Date ______________________

Ordered Pairs 1

Write the letter for each ordered pair.

A. (2, 3) ______

B. (4, 5) ______

C. (6, 4) ______

D. (1, 5) ______

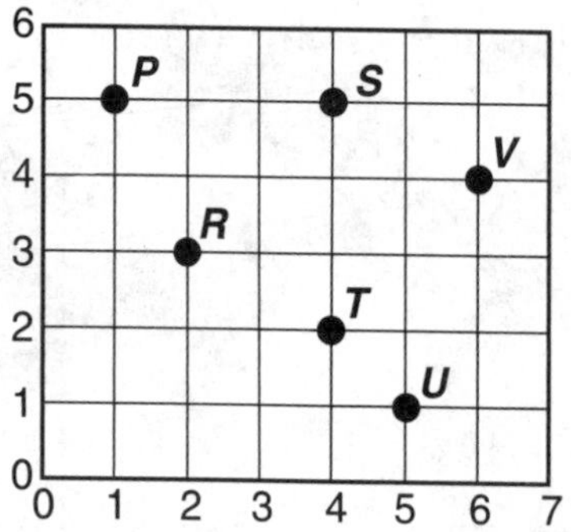

Name/Date ______________________

Ordered Pairs 2

Write the ordered pair for each point.

A ________

B ________

C ________

D ________

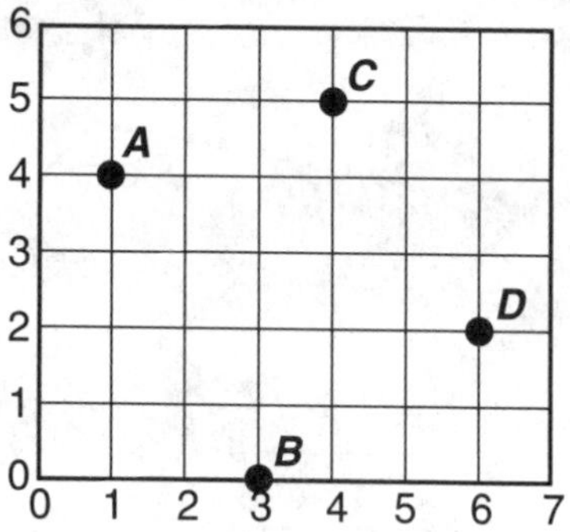

Name/Date ______________________

Ordered Pairs 3

Plot each point. Connect the points in order. Write the name of the polygon that is formed.

A. Polygon ______________

B. Polygon ______________

A.

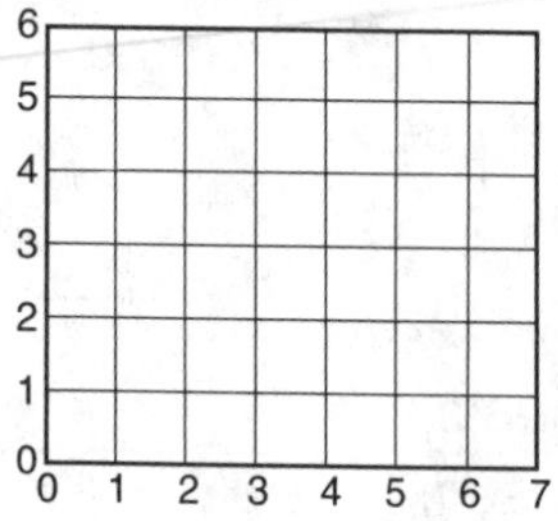

(1, 1), (3, 5), (6, 1)

B.

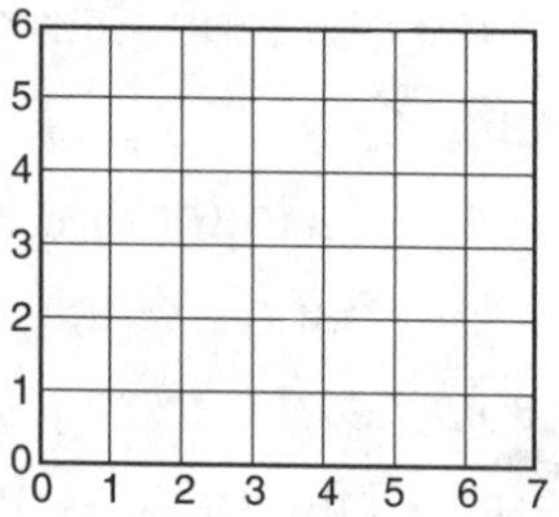

(1, 2), (1, 5), (6, 5), (6, 2)

Name/Date ______________________

Ordered Pairs 4

Write the letter for each ordered pair.

A. (2, -3) ______

B. (-1, 3) ______

C. (-2, -2) ______

D. (3, 2) ______

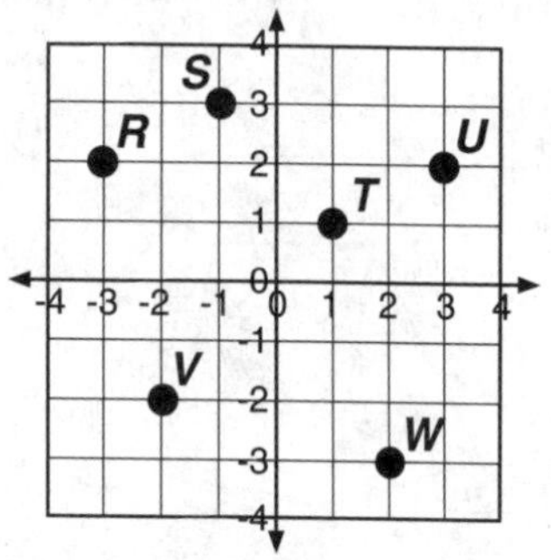

Name/Date ______________________

Ordered Pairs 5

Write the ordered pair for each point.

A ________

B ________

C ________

D ________

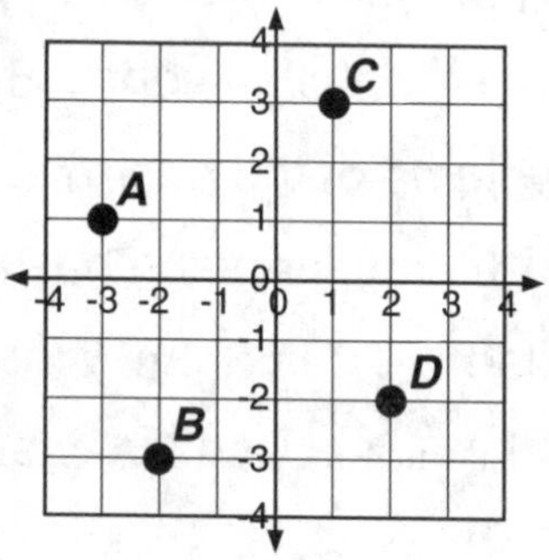

Geometry Warm-ups: Lengths on the Coordinate Plane

Name/Date ______________________

Lengths on the Coordinate Plane 1

To find the length of a horizontal line segment, find the difference of the *x*-coordinates.

$\overline{AB}$ is _____ units long.
A (**1**, 5) *B* (**4**, 5)
4 – **1** = 3

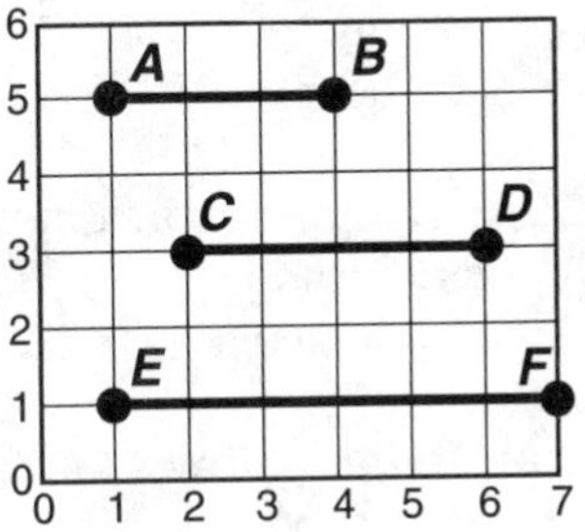

$\overline{CD}$ is _____ units long.

$\overline{EF}$ is _____ units long.

Name/Date ______________________

Lengths on the Coordinate Plane 2

To find the length of a vertical line segment, find the difference of the *y*-coordinates.

$\overline{JK}$ is _____ units long.
J (1, **5**) *J* (1, **1**)
5 – **1** = 4

$\overline{LM}$ is _____ units long.

$\overline{NO}$ is _____ units long.

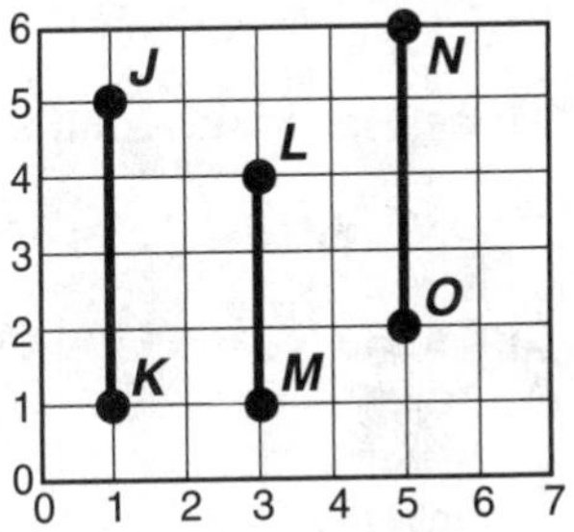

Name/Date ______________________

Lengths on the Coordinate Plane 3

Write the coordinates (ordered pairs) for each point. Then find the lengths of the segments.

A ________ *B* ________ *C* ________

D ________ *E* ________ *F* ________

$\overline{AB}$ _____ units $\overline{CD}$ _____ units $\overline{DE}$ _____ units

$\overline{AF}$ _____ units $\overline{EF}$ _____ units $\overline{BC}$ _____ units

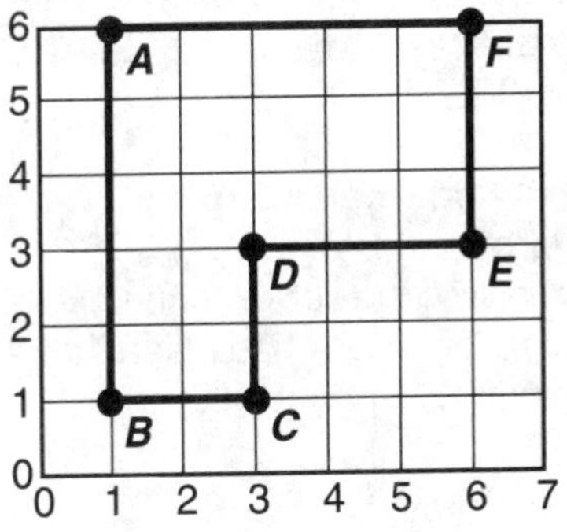

Name/Date ______________________

Lengths on the Coordinate Plane 4

A. How long is the horizontal line segment between points (0, 5) and (4, 5)? _____ units

B. How long is the vertical line segment between points (4, 8) and (4, 2)? _____ units

C. How long is the horizontal line segment between points (3, 6) and (10, 6)? _____ units

Name/Date ______________________

Lengths on the Coordinate Plane 5

A rectangle is 7 units long and 3 units wide. Two of the corners are at (10, 2) and (3, 2). What is the location of the other two corners?

____

On another sheet of paper, draw a grid and plot the points to help you.

© Mark Twain Media, Inc., Publishers

Geometry Warm-ups: Answer Keys

Lines, Rays, and Line Segments 1 (p. 2)
A. line segment
B. line
C. ray
D. ray

Lines, Rays, and Line Segments 2 (p. 2)
A. 6: $\overline{PQ}, \overline{SQ}, \overline{QR}, \overline{QT}, \overline{PR}, \overline{ST}$ (or reverse order)

Lines, Rays, and Line Segments 3 (p. 2)
A. $\overline{GH}$ or $\overline{HG}$ B. $\overrightarrow{RS}$ C. $\overrightarrow{VU}$

Lines, Rays, and Line Segments 4 (p. 2)
A. false B. false C. true D. true

Lines, Rays, and Line Segments 5 (p. 2)
A. $\overleftrightarrow{PQ}, \overleftrightarrow{TR}$ (or $\overleftrightarrow{QP}, \overleftrightarrow{RT}$) B. $\overrightarrow{SQ}, \overrightarrow{SR}, \overrightarrow{ST}, \overrightarrow{SP}, \overrightarrow{SO}$

C. $\overline{QS}, \overline{QP}$

Classifying Angles 1 (p. 3)
A. $\angle LMN$, $\angle NML$, $\angle M$ B. $\angle GEH$, $\angle HEG$, $\angle E$
C. $\angle XVZ$, $\angle ZVX$, $\angle V$

Classifying Angles 2 (p. 3)
A. vertex
B. Yes. *Y* is the vertex for both angles.
C. No. Angle *YZX* has point *Z* for a vertex rather than point *Y*.

Classifying Angles 3 (p. 3)
A. acute B. right C. straight D. obtuse

Classifying Angles 4 (p. 3)
A. right B. obtuse C. acute D. straight

Classifying Angles 5 (p. 3)
A. $\angle ABD$ or $\angle DBE$
B. $\angle ABE$ or $\angle EBC$
C. $\angle ABC$
D. $\angle DBC$

Measuring and Drawing Angles 1 (p. 4)
A. 180 B. 90 C. 90, 0 D. 90, 180

Measuring and Drawing Angles 2 (p. 4)
A. 45° B. 100° C. 120°

Measuring and Drawing Angles 3 (p. 4)
A.
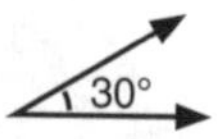

B.
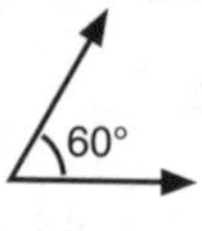

C.
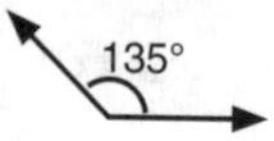

D.

Measuring and Drawing Angles 4 (p. 4)
Angles and answers will vary.

Measuring and Drawing Angles 5 (p. 4)
A. 90°, right
B. 135°, obtuse
C. 45°, acute
D. 90°, right

Classifying Pairs of Lines 1 (p. 5)
A. intersecting
B. perpendicular
C. perpendicular
D. parallel

Classifying Pairs of Lines 2 (p. 5)
Drawings should be made according to the directions. Examples:

A.
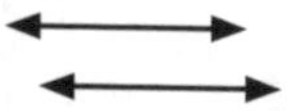
B.
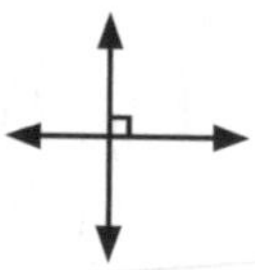
C.

Classifying Pairs of Lines 3 (p. 5)
A. $\overleftrightarrow{RS}, \overleftrightarrow{TU}$ B. $\overleftrightarrow{TU}, \overleftrightarrow{WZ}$ C. $\overleftrightarrow{RS}, \overleftrightarrow{VQ}$ or $\overleftrightarrow{TU}, \overleftrightarrow{VQ}$

Classifying Pairs of Lines 4 (p. 5)
A. T B. T C. F D. F

Classifying Pairs of Lines 5 (p. 5)
A. parallel
B. intersecting
C. perpendicular
D. parallel
E. intersecting
F. perpendicular

Special Pairs of Angles 1 (p. 6)
A. supplementary B. vertical C. complementary

Special Pairs of Angles 2 (p. 6)
A. 50° B. 45° C. 28°

Special Pairs of Angles 3 (p. 6)
A. 45° B. 123° C. 75°

Special Pairs of Angles 4 (p. 6)
A. 112 B. 83 C. 54

© Mark Twain Media, Inc., Publishers

Special Pairs of Angles 5 (p. 6)
A. 45° B. 90° C. 60°, 30° D. 95°, 85°

Identifying Polygons 1 (p. 7)
A. yes B. no C. yes D. yes
E. yes F. no

Identifying Polygons 2 (p. 7)
A. 5, 5, 5 B. 4, 4, 4 C. 8, 8, 8 D. 6, 6, 6

Identifying Polygons 3 (p. 7)
A. pentagon B. quadrilateral
C. hexagon D. octagon

Identifying Polygons 4 (p. 7)
A. No. A polygon needs at least 3 vertices to be a closed shape.
B. No. A circle is not made up of line segments.

Identifying Polygons 5 (p. 7)
A. No. A rectangle may have two pairs of sides that are different lengths.
B. Yes. A square is a special type of rectangle. All four sides are equal.

Polygon Puzzles 1 (p. 8)
A. 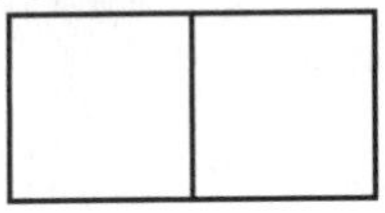
B. 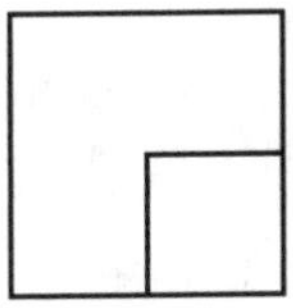

Polygon Puzzles 2 (p. 8)
A. 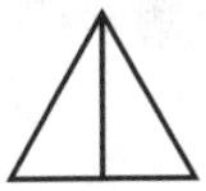
B.  or  or 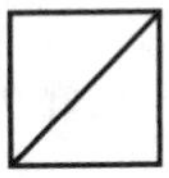

Polygon Puzzles 3 (p. 8)
There are 4 different ways to cut the rectangle in half.

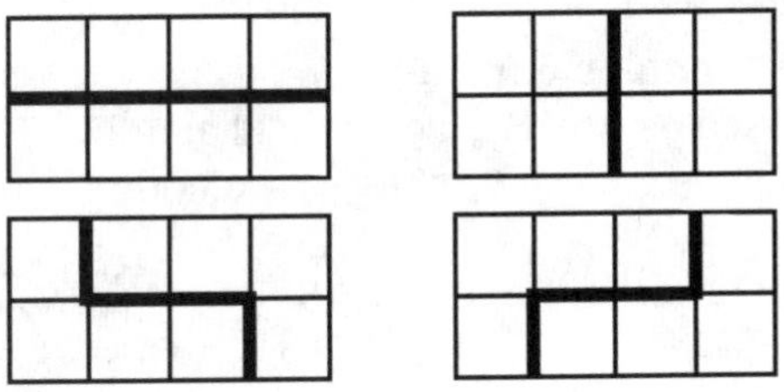

Polygon Puzzles 4 (p. 8)
There are 13 triangles: 9 small, one-cell triangles; 3 medium, four-cell triangles; and 1 large, nine-cell triangle.

Polygon Puzzles 5 (p. 8)
A. 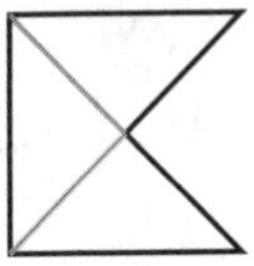
B. 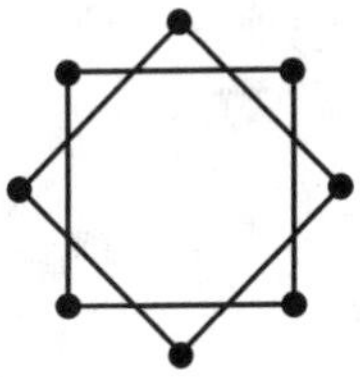

Congruent Figures 1 (p. 9)
A. no B. no C. yes D. yes

Congruent Figures 2 (p. 9)
A. 1, 3 B. 5, 6 C. 7, 8

Congruent Figures 3 (p. 9)
A. $\overline{DE}$ B. $\overline{EF}$ C. $\overline{DF}$ D. $\angle DEF$

Congruent Figures 4 (p. 9)
Examples of drawings:
A. 
B. 
C. 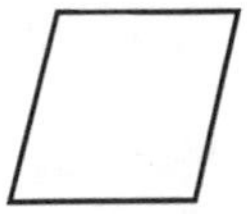

Congruent Figures 5 (p. 9)
A. Triangles *BXC, CXD, DXA* B. $\overline{BD}$ only
C. Triangles *DCB, CBA, BAD*

Similar Figures 1 (p. 10)
A. no B. yes C. yes D. no

Similar Figures 2 (p. 10)
A. 1, 2 B. 4, 6 C. 7, 8

Similar Figures 3 (p. 10)
Pairs may be listed in any order.
A. 1, 7 B. 2, 6 C. 3, 8 D. 4, 5

Similar Figures 4 (p. 10)
A. T B. F C. F D. T E. F

Similar Figures 5 (p. 10)
A. $s = 10$ B. $t = 3$ C. $x = 8, y = 6$

Symmetrical Figures 1 (p. 11)
A. yes B. no C. yes D. no

Symmetrical Figures 2 (p. 11)
A. yes 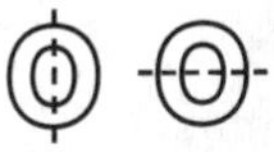 B. no C. yes 
D. no E. yes  F. yes 

Symmetrical Figures 3 (p. 11)
A. 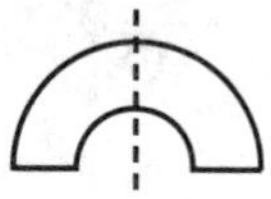 B. 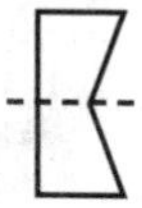 C. 
D.  E. 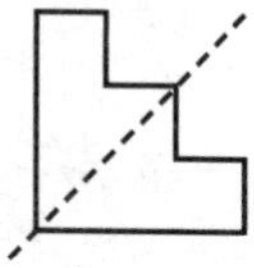

Symmetrical Figures 4 (p. 11)
A. 2 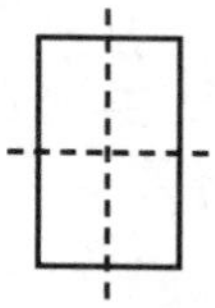 B. 4 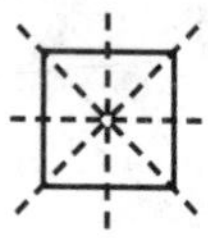 C. 3 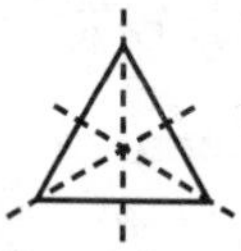

Symmetrical Figures 5 (p. 11)
A. OX B. HOE C. DID D. ICE

Two Types of Symmetry 1 (p. 12)
A. yes  B. no
C. no D. yes 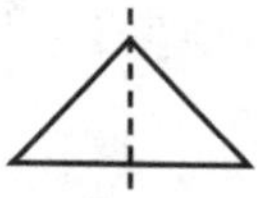

Two Types of Symmetry 2 (p. 12)
A. no B. yes C. yes D. yes

Two Types of Symmetry 3 (p. 12)
A. both B. line C. both D. both

Two Types of Symmetry 4 (p. 12)
A. line B. both C. rotational D. line

Two Types of Symmetry 5 (p. 12)
A. Drawings will vary. B. Drawings will vary.

Transformations 1 (p. 13)
A. **b** B.  C. 

Transformations 2 (p. 13)
A. 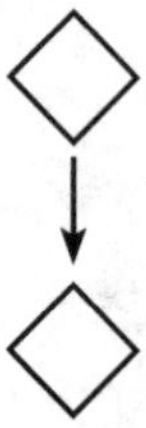 B. 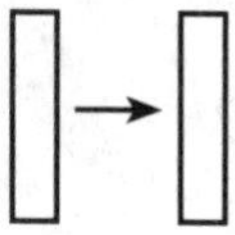 C. 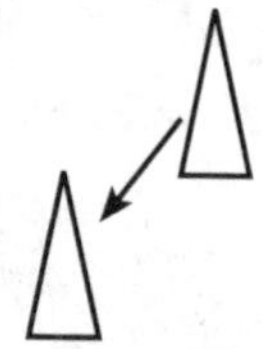

Transformations 3 (p. 13)
A.  B.  C. 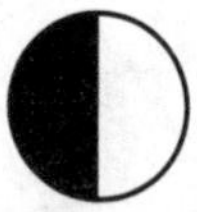

Transformations 4 (p. 13)
A. translation B. rotation C. reflection

Transformations 5 (p. 13)
A, H, I, M, O, T, U, V, W, X, Y

Geometric Patterns 1 (p. 14)
A. 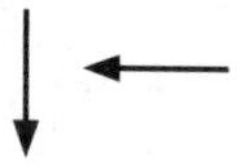 B.  C. 

Geometric Patterns 2 (p. 14)
49; The first figure is a 1 x 1 square, the second is a 2 x 2 square, and so on. The 7th figure is made up of 7 x 7 (49) squares.

Geometric Patterns 3 (p. 14)
A.–C. Teacher check patterns.
D. Patterns will vary.

Geometric Patterns 4 (p. 14)
13; The number of counters used is 3 more than the number of the figure.

Geometric Patterns 5 (p. 14)
64; (1 + 3 + 5 + 7 + 9 + 11 + 13 + 15)

Classifying Triangles 1 (p. 15)
A. isosceles B. equilateral C. scalene

Classifying Triangles 2 (p. 15)
A. right B. acute C. obtuse

Classifying Triangles 3 (p. 15)
A. scalene B. right C. isosceles D. acute

Classifying Triangles 4 (p. 15)
A. S B. A C. S D. N

Classifying Triangles 5 (p. 15)
A. right, isosceles B. acute, equilateral
C. right, scalene D. obtuse, scalene

Classifying Quadrilaterals 1 (p. 16)
A. yes B. no C. yes D. yes
E. no F. yes

Classifying Quadrilaterals 2 (p. 16)
2, 5, 7, 8

Classifying Quadrilaterals 3 (p. 16)
A. 5, 7 B. 2, 7 C. 4, 6 D. 2, 3, 5, 7
E. 1, 2, 3, 4, 5, 6, 7

© Mark Twain Media, Inc., Publishers

Classifying Quadrilaterals 4 (p. 16)
Teacher check drawings.
A. Drawing should be of a trapezoid.
B. Drawing should be of a rhombus or square.
C. Drawing should be of a rectangle or square.

Classifying Quadrilaterals 5 (p. 16)
A. Yes. A square is a rhombus that has four right angles.
B. No. Quadrilaterals have to have four sides, but the sides do not need to be parallel.

Classifying Parallelograms 1 (p. 17)
A. yes B. no C. yes D. yes
E. yes F. no

Classifying Parallelograms 2 (p. 17)
A. rhombus, square B. rectangle, square
C. rhombus, rectangle, square

Classifying Parallelograms 3 (p. 17)
A. Yes. All rectangles have opposite sides that are congruent and parallel.
B. No. Some quadrilaterals have no parallel sides. Some have parallel sides that aren't congruent.

Classifying Parallelograms 4 (p. 17)
A. $\overline{EF}$ and $\overline{GH}$, $\overline{EG}$ and $\overline{FH}$
B. $\overline{EF}$ and $\overline{GH}$, $\overline{EG}$ and $\overline{FH}$

Classifying Parallelograms 5 (p. 17)
QXZW, XRYZ, WZVT, ZYSV, QXVT, XRSV, QRYW, WYST

Angle Measures of Triangles 1 (p. 18)
A. 180
B. If a triangle had two right angles, the sum of the three angle measures would be greater than 180 degrees.

Angle Measures of Triangles 2 (p. 18)
A. $\angle D$ B. 80° C. 45°

Angle Measures of Triangles 3 (p. 18)
A. 30° B. 25° C. 50° D. 125°

Angle Measures of Triangles 4 (p. 18)
A. 40° B. 25° C. 48° D. 55°

Angle Measures of Triangles 5 (p. 18)
A. 45° B. 60° C. 60°, 30°

Angle Measures of Quadrilaterals 1 (p. 19)
A. 360
B. If it had more than three obtuse angles, the sum of the angle measures would be greater than 360 degrees.

Angle Measures of Quadrilaterals 2 (p. 19)
A. $\angle R$ B. 75° C. 180°

Angle Measures of Quadrilaterals 3 (p. 19)
A. 80° B. 55° C. 125° D. 127°

Angle Measures of Quadrilaterals 4 (p. 19)
A. 60° B. 90° C. 62° D. 105°

Angle Measures of Quadrilaterals 5 (p. 19)
$\angle A = 60°$ $\angle B = 120°$ $\angle C = 60°$ $\angle D = 120°$

Perimeter of Rectangles and Squares 1 (p. 20)
A. 10 B. 24 C. 8

Perimeter of Rectangles and Squares 2 (p. 20)
A. 28 feet B. 44 inches C. 48 meters

Perimeter of Rectangles and Squares 3 (p. 20)
Teacher check rectanges. Measurements should be:
3 in. by 4 in.; 2 in. by 5 in.; 6 in. by 1 in.

Perimeter of Rectangles and Squares 4 (p. 20)
A. 3 cm B. 4 ft.
C. length = 11 m; width = 5 m

Perimeter of Rectangles and Squares 5 (p. 20)
A. 24 ft., 8 yd. B. 144 in., 12 ft.

Perimeter of Polygons 1 (p. 21)
A. 12 B. 18 C. 28

Perimeter of Polygons 2 (p. 21)
A. 30 B. 48 C. 54

Perimeter of Polygons 3 (p. 21)
A. 36 in., 3 ft. B. 24 in., 2 ft. C. 288 in., 24 ft.

Perimeter of Polygons 4 (p. 21)
A. 6 cm B. 9 ft. C. 7 m

Perimeter of Polygons 5 (p. 21)
A. 2 B. 4 C. 1, 3

Perimeter of Complex Figures 1 (p. 22)
A. 20 B. 26

Perimeter of Complex Figures 2 (p. 22)
A. 24 B. 34

Perimeter of Complex Figures 3 (p. 22)
A = 8 m B = 7 m Perimeter = 30 m

Perimeter of Complex Figures 4 (p. 22)
A. 31 B. $62.00

Perimeter of Complex Figures 5 (p. 22)
A = 12 m; Perimeter = 38 m
B = 9 in.; Perimeter = 34 in.
C = 2 ft.; Perimeter = 30 ft.

Area of Rectangles and Squares 1 (p. 23)
A. 96 B. 49 C. 27

Area of Rectangles and Squares 2 (p. 23)
A. 180 ft.^{2} B. 38 in.

Area of Rectangles and Squares 3 (p. 23)
Teacher check drawings. There should be a 3 x 3 square and a 5 x 1 rectangle.
The 3 x 3 square has the greatest area.

Area of Rectangles and Squares 4 (p. 23)
A. 36 in.^{2} B. 11 cm C. 1 yd.^{2}

Area of Rectangles and Squares 5 (p. 23)
A. 8 inches, 4 inches B. 49 in.^{2}

Area of Triangles 1 (p. 24)
A. 28 yd.^{2} B. 30 yd.^{2} C. 50 yd.^{2} D. C

Area of Triangles 2 (p. 24)
A. 6 B. 24

Area of Triangles 3 (p. 24)
A. 12 B. 60

Area of Triangles 4 (p. 24)
A. ½*su* B. ½*xy*

Area of Triangles 5 (p. 24)
A. 8 cm B. 12 ft.

Area of Parallelograms 1 (p. 25)
A. 108 B. 40 C. 54

Area of Parallelograms 2 (p. 25)
A. 32 B. 15

Area of Parallelograms 3 (p. 25)
A. 80 B. 72 C. 77 D. A E. B

Area of Parallelograms 4 (p. 25)
A. 6 cm B. 84 in.^{2} C. 13 ft.

Area of Parallelograms 5 (p. 25)
length—10 cm area—80 cm^2

Area of Complex Figures 1 (p. 26)
A. 19
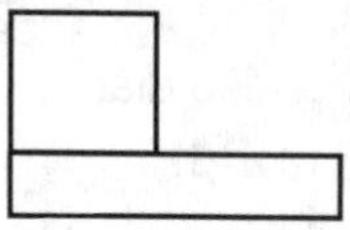
or
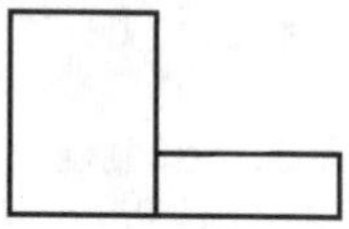

B. 58
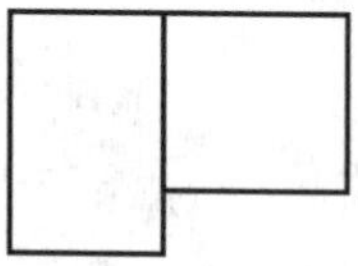
or
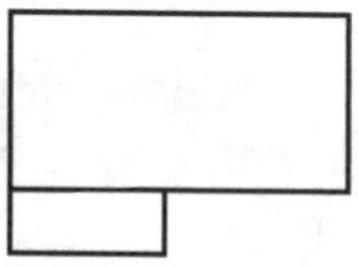

C. 60
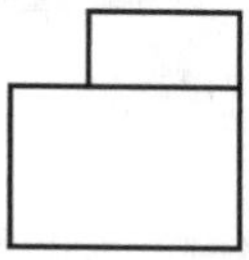
or
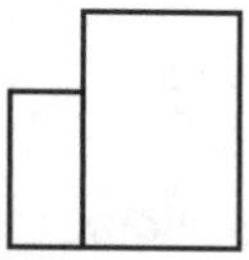

Area of Complex Figures 2 (p. 26)
48

Area of Complex Figures 3 (p. 26)
x = 12 ft. y = 15 ft. Area = 94 ft.^{2}

Area of Complex Figures 4 (p. 26)
x = 12 yd. y = 5 yd. P = 50 yd.
A = 92 yd.^{2}

Area of Complex Figures 5 (p. 26)
x = 5 in. y = 3 in. P = 46 in. A = 65 in.^{2}

Area of Irregular Regions 1 (p. 27)
A. 13 (10 whole squares and 6 half-squares)
B. 9 (6 whole squares and 6 half-squares)

Area of Irregular Regions 2 (p. 27)
6 ½ (1 whole square and 11 half-squares)

Area of Irregular Regions 3 (p. 27)
17.5 (9 whole squares and 17 half-squares)

Area of Irregular Regions 4 (p. 27)
Shape and area will vary.

Area of Irregular Regions 5 (p. 27)
Area will vary.

Circles 1 (p. 28)
A. center B. radius C. chord D. diameter

Circles 2 (p. 28)
Example:
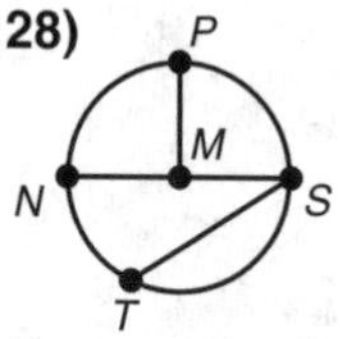

Circles 3 (p. 28)
A. $\overline{EG}$, $\overline{HJ}$ B. point F
C. $\overline{HK}$ D. $\overline{EF}$, $\overline{FG}$, $\overline{HF}$, $\overline{FJ}$

Circles 4 (p. 28)
A. radius B. chord (also diameter)
C. semicircle D. diameter

Circles 5 (p. 28)
A. 3 cm B. 3 cm C. 6 cm
D. Multiply the length of the radius by 2.

Circles and Central Angles 1 (p. 29)
A. $\angle CBD$ B. $\angle ABD$

Circles and Central Angles 2 (p. 29)
A. 180° B. 90° C. 90°

Circles and Central Angles 3 (p. 29)
A. S B. A C. N D. A

Circles and Central Angles 4 (p. 29)
Example:

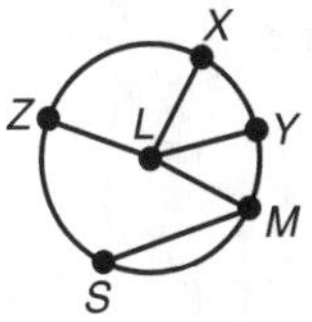

Circles and Central Angles 5 (p. 29)
A.

B.

Circumference 1 (p. 30)
A. perimeter B. three C. $\pi \times d$

Circumference 2 (p. 30)
A. 44 B. 66

Circumference 3 (p. 30)
A. 12.56 B. 31.4

Circumference 4 (p. 30)
A. 25.12 cm B. 15.7 ft. C. 9 in.

Circumference 5 (p. 30)
A. 21.98 cm or 22 cm B. 62.8 ft. or $62\frac{6}{7}$ ft.
C. 37.68 in. or $37\frac{5}{7}$ in.

Area of Circles 1 (p. 31)
A. 314 B. 28.26

Area of Circles 2 (p. 31)
A. 154 B. $314\frac{2}{7}$

Area of Circles 3 (p. 31)
A. 78.5 B. 1,256

Area of Circles 4 (p. 31)
A. Divide the circumference by 3.14 to find the diameter. Divide the diameter by 2 to find the radius. Square the radius and multiply by 3.14.
B. 314 m^2

Area of Circles 5 (p. 31)
Answers will vary.

Solid Figures 1 (p. 32)
A. cylinder B. square pyramid
C. rectangular prism D. cone

Solid Figures 2 (p. 32)
A. yes B. yes C. no D. yes
E. yes

Solid Figures 3 (p. 32)
A. 6 B. 1 C. 6 D. 5
E. 2

Solid Figures 4 (p. 32)
A. 12 edges, 8 vertices B. 8 edges, 5 vertices
C. 6 edges, 4 vertices D. 12 edges, 8 vertices

Solid Figures 5 (p. 32)
A. S B. A C. A D. N

Solid Figures and Nets 1 (p. 33)
A. cube B. square pyramid C. rectangular prism

Solid Figures and Nets 2 (p. 33)
A.

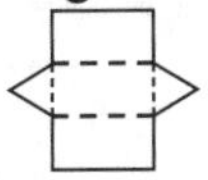

B.

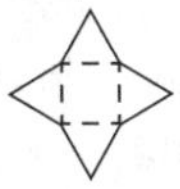

Solid Figures and Nets 3 (p. 33)
Examples:

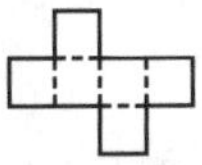

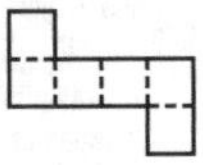

Solids and Nets 4 (p. 33)
A. The nets have the same number of faces.
B. All the faces of the cube's net are congruent, but those of other rectangular prisms aren't.

Solid Figures and Nets 5 (p. 33)
A

Surface Area of Rectangular Prisms 1 (p. 34)
384

Surface Area of Rectangular Prisms 2 (p. 34)
126

© Mark Twain Media, Inc., Publishers

Surface Area of Rectangular Prisms 3 (p. 34)
A. 126 B. 92 C. 96 D. A

Surface Area of Rectangular Prisms 4 (p. 34)
150 $in.^2$

Surface Area of Rectangular Prisms 5 (p. 34)

Sides of Cube	Surface Area
1	6
2	24
4	96
8	384

The surface area becomes four times greater.

Volume of Rectangular Prisms 1 (p. 35)
80 cubes
Accept any reasonable explanation. Example: I multiplied 4 x 4 and then multiplied that by 5.

Volume of Rectangular Prisms 2 (p. 35)
A. 27 B. 125

Volume of Rectangular Prisms 3 (p. 35)
A. 21 B. 320

Volume of Rectangular Prisms 4 (p. 35)
Box A has the greater volume.
A. 210 B. 192

Volume of Rectangular Prisms 5 (p. 35)
A. 6 ft. B. 4 cm C. 8 $in.^3$

Volume of Cylinders 1 (p. 36)
A. $B = 3.14\ m^2$, $V = 18.84\ m^3$
B. $B = 50.24\ in.^2$, $V = 200.96\ in.^3$

Volume of Cylinders 2 (p. 36)
A. circle B. area C. height D. cubic

Volume of Cylinders 3 (p. 36)
B has the greater volume.
A. $B = 12.56\ m^2$, $V = 75.36\ m^3$
B. $B = 28.26\ m^2$, $V = 113.04\ m^3$

Volume of Cylinders 4 (p. 36)
A. 3,140 cm^3 B. 785 cm^3

Volume of Cylinders 5 (p. 36)
A. 28.26 $yd.^2$
B. Accept any reasonable explanation. Example: I divided the volume by the height to get 28.26 square yards.

Volume of Triangular Prisms 1 (p. 37)
A. $B = 3\ in.^2$, $V = 18\ in.^3$
B. $B = 32\ m^2$, $V = 224\ m^3$

Volume of Triangular Prisms 2 (p. 37)
A. triangle B. ½ C. height

Volume of Triangular Prisms 3 (p. 37)
$B = 54\ cm^2$, $V = 270\ cm^3$

Volume of Triangular Prisms 4 (p. 37)
A. 70 $in.^3$ B. 18 cm^2

Volume of Triangular Prisms 5 (p. 37)
B has the greater volume. A. 96 cm^3 B. 120 cm^3

Ordered Pairs 1 (p. 38)
A. R B. S C. V D. P

Ordered Pairs 2 (p. 38)
A (1, 4) B (3, 0) C (4, 5) D (6, 2)

Ordered Pairs 3 (p. 38)
A. triangle

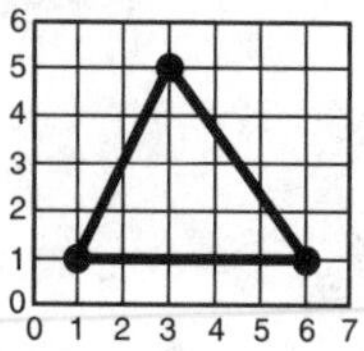

B. rectangle

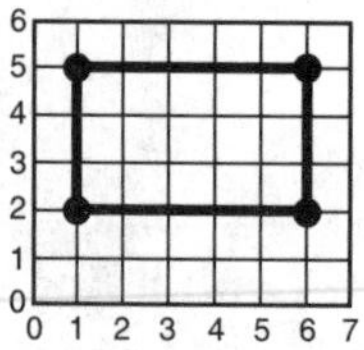

Ordered Pairs 4 (p. 38)
A. W B. S C. V D. U

Ordered Pairs 5 (p. 38)
A. (-3, 1) B. (-2, -3) C. (1, 3) D. (2, -2)

Lengths on a Coordinate Plane 1 (p. 39)
$\overline{AB} = 3$ $\overline{CD} = 4$ $\overline{EF} = 6$

Lengths on a Coordinate Plane 2 (p. 39)
$\overline{JK} = 4$ $\overline{LM} = 3$ $\overline{NO} = 4$

Lengths on a Coordinate Plane 3 (p. 39)
A (1, 6) B (1, 1) C (3, 1) D (3, 3)
E (6, 3) F (6, 6)
$\overline{AB} = 5$ $\overline{AF} = 5$ $\overline{CD} = 2$ $\overline{EF} = 3$
$\overline{DE} = 3$ $\overline{BC} = 2$

Lengths on a Coordinate Plane 4 (p. 39)
A. 4 B. 6 C. 7

Lengths on a Coordinate Plane 5 (p. 39)
(3, 5) and (10, 5)

© Mark Twain Media, Inc., Publishers